Above: Firthcliffe station sign, in a private collection since the 1950's

Cover photo and below: NYO&W Train No. 1 near Firthcliffe with Ten-Wheeler No. 227 on 3-23-1946.
These images are from the Donald W. Furler Collection at the Center for Railroad Photography & Art.
Alan Furler

#227 and her three sisters were called "teakettles"
1911 vintage, they were loved by crew and observer alike for their handling, their looks and speed. On a straight stretch of track these ladies could dance with the best of them!

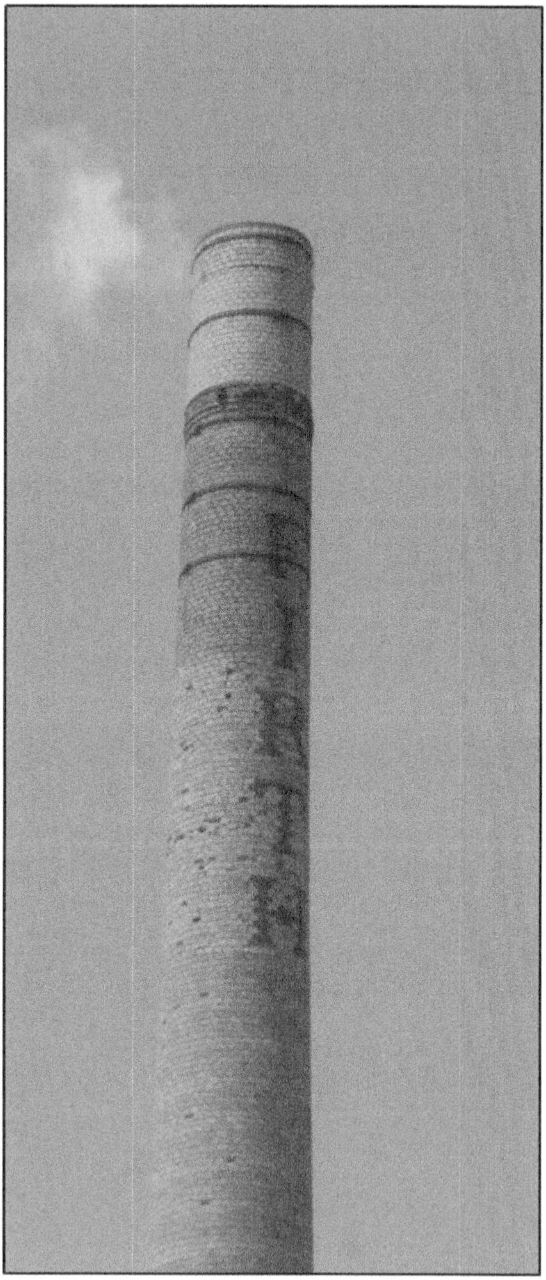

Table of Contents

Foreword/My many thanks to......................5
1873- 1963..10
Firth Honor Roll...17
Dedication..19
"Roll on Moodna"/History, Honor
And Murder on the Moodna...........................21
Chapter 1-The early years...............................33
Chapter 2-Out and about................................51
Chapter 3-The flood of 1903...........................59
Chapter 4-Firtcliffe Station and "tunnel"........69
Chapter 5-Fithcliffe Clubhouse........................97
Chapter 6-The Aqueduct................................111
Chapter 7-OrrsMills/Orrs Mills North.............117
Chapter 8-World War One..............................147
Chapter 9-Between the wars..........................155
Chapter 10-World War Two............................177
Chapter Eleven-Postwar years/Growing up
in Firthcliffe by Edward
Smith..191
Chapter 12...... A hammer built the railroad
....203
Chapter 13-Firth Carpet in the last years.........219
Chapter 14-Moodna Farewell..........................255
Epilogue..259

ISBN #
9781478206330

Sir Thomas Freeman Firth [1829-1909]

Sir Algernon Freeman Firth [1856-1936]

Photos: Online Search

Foreword/My Many Thanks To…

Firth Carpet Company, and its namesake town of Firthcliffe, is both a typical and a classic American story. It's America at the height of its manufacturing might, its immigrants coming to start a new life in a new land. However, where so many mills and factories offered little more than a daily wage, Firth Carpet was offering a clubhouse with all the modern facilities. Where thousands of workers were living in tenements, Firth employees were offered modern housing to rent, with a backyard garden, and someone on site to till the ground.

And then in the end, Firth became another Story of America's industrial decline, decaying buildings littering the landscape. In 2012, I was one of those who watched in disbelief as fire tore through the old Firth complex. Surely, dozens that were there that cold January day, videotaping the blaze, knew little or nothing of Firth Carpet. But those of us who knew otherwise, could only watch as a part of our family history vanished window by window, rooftop by rooftop.

It's been a century and a half since the Firths first set up shop (apparently with some misgivings to the outcome) in an abandoned woolen mill along the banks of Moodna creek. It's been seven years since the fire; and a decade since I wrote this book's first edition. To backtrack now across the years, I owe countless thanks to the following:

Mr.& Mrs. John Staples, Mr. Staples was the mill electrician; Michael William Raab (Firthcliffe), John (Jack) Arnott (Firthcliffe) Lynn McCarthy (Firthcliffe) John Gilardo, Billy Shovan, Irene Sheldon,

Doug Spaulding (Firthcliffe) and a special thanks to Edwin Smith, whose first-hand reminisces of growing up in Firthcliffe, bring back the feel of a genuine company town.

From the Ontario and Western Railway Historical Society: Ray Kelly, Walter Kierzkowski, Jeff Otto, Ron Vassallo, Joe Bux
Thank you to Alan Furler, and The Center for Railroad Photography & Art, for access to the David Furler Photograph Collection.

Sadly, two dear friends who were such an influence on this book are gone now: George Kane and Ed Crist, both characters in their own right. I had the pleasure of exploring the old Firth complex with George Kane, the Firthcliffe historian. George's generosity in his sharing of family pictures, and his enthusiasm for the old mill, were unmatched.

In writing the first book, I also had the honor of meeting for the first time Edward J. Crist: A former Lehigh and Hudson River Railroad employee; author, and historian. An industrial engineer by profession, Ed's field of writing was mostly railroading. But there wasn't a topic you couldn't ask him about without getting a solid, honest answer. Ed grew up in Firthcliffe, just yards from the old train station. By bittersweet luck he was home from college that early morning the station he knew so well from childhood burned to the ground.

He was there in the Ontario and Western Railway's final years, no coincidence that, that was the name of his first published railroad book. The start of a series of railroad books that would influence a generation of railfans who know the glory days of railroading only secondhand.

His support of my new work, as well as the support of his wife, Stella and her generosity for my access to her husband's incredible photo collection, helped make this work possible. *Highland Mills, July, 2019*

1942: Firth Carpet ceremony for employees with 25 years or more of service. Sitting L to R: Harold Brown, Harrison O'Dell, William Wells, William Keator, Edson Hallock, William Sullivan, Edward Babcock, Floyd Sullivan, Robert Arnott Sr., James Richardson, Andy Lee Sr., Norman Goodall, Jacob Keator and James Wormald. Standing L to R: Robert Nelson Sr., Nelson Smith Sr., Ernest Smith Sr., George Smith, John B. Arnott, John Brunton, Norman Stewart, Ralph Weeks, Edward F. Burton, Elmer Young, Russell R. Matthews, Claude Keator, William Sinclair, John Thompson, Bertha Woolsey, Mollie Quinlin, Lulu Woolsey, Agnes Mitchell, Alex Sharp, Victor Winfield and Ephriam Staples. — *George Kane*

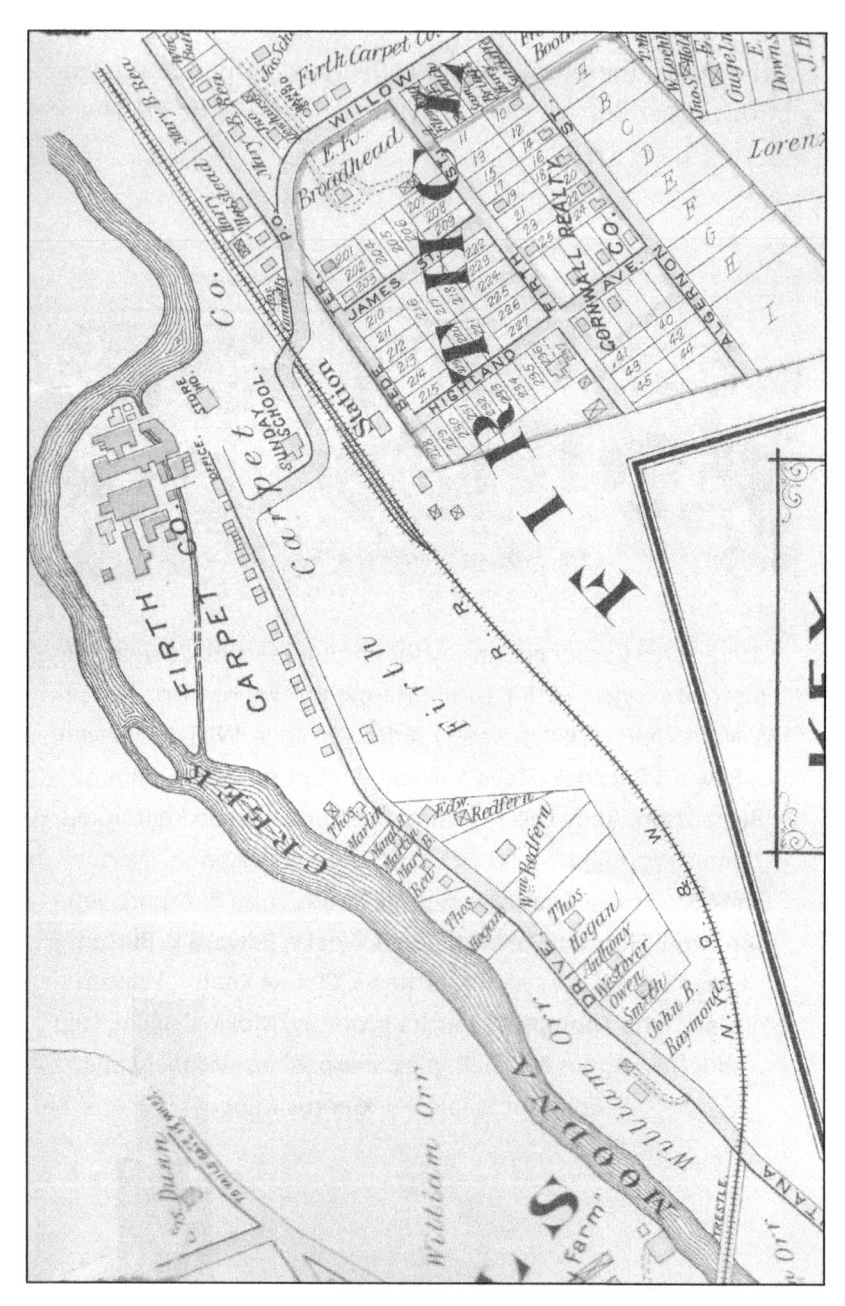

1903 Mueller's Orange County Atlas

Early postcard view of Firth Carpet, about 1915
"Coming down the hill, from left to right, skein* drying room, drum room, with the mixed colors room in the rear; back of this is the spinning and carding room, the lower part which was used for skein winding, center forward, cop boiling room, with loom wire making above. In back is the weave shop and print winding, cop winding and beam department on the first floor, at extreme right is the storage shed for bamboo poles and other materials and the large building was used for the weave shop, cut order and finishing room." Harrison O'Dell, *Cornwall Local*

Firthcliffe station and O&W train in the background, left

1873 and 1963

Lewis Beach

Farmer, Lawyer, politician, Cornwall Supervisor, U.S. Representative from New York representing two different congressional districts. In 1873 he wrote what is still considered today the finest history of Cornwall

Born March 30, 1835, in New York, NY; Died: August 10, 1886, in Cornwall

Upon his death his fellow politicians wrote for his eulogy:

"He always had a pleasant word for any one, and never spoke a harsh word except in denunciation of an act of wrong or injustice. In his domestic relations he was beloved as a husband and father, and his whole time was divided between his devotion to his family and to his official duties. He knew no pleasure or enjoyment beyond them.

Among his immediate friends and neighbors Mr. Beach was warmly esteemed. The triple life that he led of farmer, lawyer, and legislator brought him into close relation with all classes of people, and all found in him a ready and willing counselor and friend. He possessed an intuitive knowledge of the wants of his constituents, and the humblest among them never sought his advice or assistance in vain."

A decade before the railroad arrived in Firthcliffe, Beach wrote of Orrs Mills and Montana:

"The first in order of place to utilize this power are the grist mills of J&W Orr, located a short distance from the north of Townsend bridge. The site now occupied by the mills, was, from a very early day, used for a similar purpose. In 1864 the old mill was taken down and the Messrs. Orr, erected the present buildings, which for convenience, commodiousness, and perfection of machinery, are equal to any in the country.

Not far from the Orr establishment are the Painters mills, now in disuse. They were built a few years since with a view of manufacturing paint from a peculiar stone convenient to the spot. After a brief experiment, operations were suspended, and they have since remained idle. The property is now owned by Thomas Dumville.

As we follow the Moodna towards its mouth we next come upon the Cornwall Woolen-Mills. In 1869 these mills came under the management of F.W. Broadhead, a gentleman of long experience in the manufacture of woolens. About 125 hands find employment here, and the works are carried on by both steam and water power.

To reach the Woolen Mills, you take Willow Avenue at Canterbury, and continue on until the brow of Montana Hill is reached. In the deep glen before you, confined on all sides from towering hills, nestles the hamlet, Montana. To the extreme north, half hid by the intervening slope, stand the Woolen-mills. You descend the hill which is remarkably steep, and s slight detour to the right brings you to the gate of the mills. At the foot of Montana Hill the road makes an abrupt turn to the south-so abrupt as to cause a doubt of it's being a distinct road of itself, or merely a continuation of Willow Avenue. To dispel the doubt, we may say Willow Avenue terminates at the top of Montana Hill, from that point to Townsend bridge, the road takes the name of Montana Drive. This is one of the most picturesque drives in Cornwall. The road, which is constantly ascending, is skirted by immense pines and spruces, through which now and then is gained a glimpse of the Moodna, tumbling and roaring in the gorge below, scores of feet away. As the Townsend bridge comes in sight, a spot is reached from which a most enchanting view is to be had. It has frequently challenged the admiration of prominent artists who have visited Cornwall"

Townsend's bridge: Then and now

George Kane

UP THE HILL, Firthcliffe, N. Y.

Top of Montana hill, with the station visible to the left

Anna's Store[1] and Post office to the right

---

[1] Growing up in Firthcliffe by Edward Smith, page 191

1963:

STATION BURNS—Flames roar out of doomed New York, Ontario and Western Railroad station during early morning fire which destroyed 75-year-old structure at Firthcliffe. Station had been abandoned since railroad company folded six years ago.

Photo by Alan Conover

September 18th, 1963: The O&W's Firthcliffe station is the target of an arsonist.
There had smaller fires in the building prior to this, but this one proved to be the fatal blow. This is from the copy of the edition of the Newburgh's Evening News from Ed Crist's collection.. This edition is so fascinating and poignant both historically and personally, because one of the firemen in the picture is my grandfather, Martin, who grew up around this station.

Going through the whole paper, there is such a cross section of events that were going at that the time: The tragic church bombing in Birmingham; riots, protests, a political cartoon on segregation, and Con Ed was beginning work on the hydroelectric plant on Storm King mountain, and with it the beginning of a 20-year environmental battle that would rewrite environmental history.

And it was only two months before
President Kennedy took that fateful trip to Dallas.

The times they were a changing....

THE FIFTH NEWS
CARPET COMPANY

Vol. V   JUNE, 1943   No. 11

Our First Casualty

Private Ralph Cassidy is the first of our boys from Firth, that we know of, who has earned the Purple Heart. He was wounded in action in the North African area April 8, 1943, but is now in a hospital and on the road to recovery and further service.

Private Cassidy enlisted in the army in September, 1940, and served at Fort Dix until September 1941, when he received an honorable discharge. He was again inducted in June, 1942, and received his basic training at Fort McClellan, Alabama, and was then sent overseas in September of that same year. After spending a short time in Ireland he was sent to Africa where he is at the present time.

Prior to his induction he worked in the Finishing Department among his many friends. He was also employed in our Axminster Setting Department at one time.

George Kane

Firth Honor Roll

Mr. & Mrs. John Staples

Column one

Thayer, R. Jr.; Janetti, P.P.; Middleton, M.; Turner, G.W.; Shanley, J.F.; Brennan, S.; Brown, G. Jr.; Orsini, R.; Smith, J.J.; Rolan, F.; Fitzpatrick, T.; Pike, J.; Welsh, M.G.; Arnott, R.B.; Snyder, H.; McCutcheon, I; Groves, G; Callahan, J.; Morrison, K.; Rorvell, F.; Rhodes, K.; Barnum, G; Elwood, D.; Dowry, A.; Joulio, C.M. ; Barberi, S.; Thayer, R.; Barley, R.; **Cassidy, R**.; Smith, S.F.; Ruff, W. Jr.; Hughes, R.; Alexander, R.; McGrath, T.; Morrison, J.T.; Harris, A.; Culler, R.; Swenson, W.G.; Stawdesky, A.; Lancles, A.; Tompkins, P.B.; Craig, W.S.; Murphy, R.B. ; Bardin, J.P.; Bloom, W.; Tulle, R.; Wilmarth, C.; Smith, V.; Glenn, J.

Column two

Hannigan, J.; Marshall, H.; Gilardo, S.; Stevenson, R.; Downsbrough, H.; Warden, S.; Whitman, M.; Kuratz, S.; Burger, W.C.; Terwilliger, H.; Kirk, M.W.; Mcarthy, S.; Terwilliger, S.; Palmer, K.B.; Hulse, H.F.; Sharples, S.C.; Speder, A.S.; Steffens, M.K.; Derocco, V.J.; Sanseveri, D.; Rolan, J.R.; Moroney, S.; Howard, R.R.; Cuphers, G.Y.; Hunter, J.C.; Fowler, L.G.; Kahn, W.J.; Martin, J.; Matagora, S.C.; Staples, S.; Quigley, F.P.; McCartney, M.J.; Burle, R.J.; Kenning, S.; Joulio, D.; Anderson, R.; Brewer, J; Morrison, G.; Oneil, J.H.; McGuiness, J.W.; Jones, C; Roche, J.G.; Cox, W.; Staples, O.P.; Chamberlin, P,; Ladik, J.; Becker, F.; Judson, P.M.; Warden, M.; Ketcham, D.R.; Retson, R. Jr.; McCullough, P.

Column three

Fredricks, K.A.; Callahan, M.; Raab, G.W.; Vrandenburgh, F.; DeMiceli, C.; Reeks, I.H.; Bukouski, D.A.; O'Dell, M.R.; Rupert, D.; Shearer, J.S.; Wylan, R.; Everitt, S.; Lixfield, T.;

Wilson, C.; Feller, W.F. Jr.; Post, P.J.; McKinstry,P.; Kent, J.; Schoonmaker, M.; Pryne, W.; Stratton,, C.; Carey, W.D.; Keegan, J.F.

To my Father and Jeannie

"When someone you love becomes
a memory, the memory
becomes a treasure."

~Author Unknown

Taken in the early 1900s, this picture was submitted by Burt Young. Front row, from left, is: nknown, Bill Prause, Hobart Pierse, and Frederick Pierse. The second row, is from left, Cyril earwood, and Morris Pierse. The back row is, from left, a Prause, John Laurie, unknown, lem LaBarr, unknown, and Walt Worden.

Both, Cornwall Historical Society

"Roll on Moodna, ye eternal waters race"

Water: we have no qualms about harnessing it for our own use. We drink it from a well laid out series of pipes. We clean with it, we swim in it. With a dam we harness water to make the electricity that sustains our lives. But this same water, when not being handled with the proper respect it commands, can turn on us with disastrous results. Water in a boiler, when heated with fire, creates a power capable of hurtling hundreds of tons of steel down a track at speeds in excess of one hundred miles an hour. But a boiler that is not given enough water will explode and horribly scald, maim and kill without any regard to whomever or whatever is within range. Water from a broken pipe can wreak major havoc on our daily routine. But water escaping from an overflowing creek bank or from a collapsing dam has the power to cause destruction on a biblical scale.

For centuries creek banks were lined with mills of every size and description, harnessing the power of the water for their own purposes. The water kept the mills alive but the mill owners did not return the favor in kind, leaving in their passing waterways so polluted as to be given up for dead. The great industrial age that had made these mills has vanished. The few of these mills themselves that still survive are shadows of their former selves. But as it has for eons, the water goes on its way. A movement to remove old dams is in full flower. Getting the waters themselves clean and keeping them that way for all time are battles that rise and fall on the tide of modern politics.

(Story continues on page 250)

History, Murder and Honor on the Moodna

What we know as Moodna Creek has its point of origin Cromline Creek, near present-day Chester. Along its nineteen-mile trek it picks up the waters of Otterkill, Woodbury and Idlewild Creek. At the end of its journey the Moodna connects with the waters of the mighty Hudson River near what is today Cornwall-on-Hudson. From there it's a fifty-odd mile trip south to the great city and the vast Atlantic Ocean beyond. That is the physical Moodna.

The other Moodna Creek, the one of legend and lore, goes back nearly four centuries to a family of settlers named Stacey who met their horrible fate at the hands of Indians near present-day Cornwall, The following paragraphs pick up the story:

"Three centuries back, a settler named Stacy, his wife and two children, a old son and a three year old daughter, built a cabin at the mouth of Moodna Creek. They were good neighbors to the Indians inhabiting the area, and soon became close friends with an elderly man of the tribe named Naoman.

One day Naoman visited Mrs. Stacy, obviously very troubled. Mrs. Stacy swore secrecy, and Naoman told her that the white man had insulted the Indians, and that his tribe was about to murder every white settler in the area. Mrs. Stacy went to find her husband, who was out fishing in the Hudson River at the time, to tell him what she had learned.

Time was precious, and valuable minutes were lost as Stacy rowed into shore, bailed out his boat, grabbed his children and rifle. A young buck of the tribe who had been suspicious of Naomi's visits with the Stacy's, saw what was happening and ran to the Indian Village to give the alert.

Meanwhile, Stacy had managed to row out into the Hudson, when he was overtaken by Indian canoes. He was escorted ashore with his family, and watched silently as the tribe burned his cabin to the ground.

The tribal chief realized that someone had given the alarm to Stacy and his family, and he sought the name of the traitor. Stacy would say nothing, so the chief promised Mrs. Stacy he would kill her children if she did not confess who it was. As the chief was about to kill the daughter, Naomi stepped forward and told of his friendship with the white settlers and of his act of treason in warning them. Naomi's punishment was swift and instantaneous: he fell dead with a hatchet in his head. The same tragic fate would befell the Stacy's. Forever after these clear running waters, which had yet to know little change at the hand of man, would be known as "Murderers Creek". The very name "Moodna" would come from the Dutch word "Moordenaars" or "Murderers".

Writer Nathaniel P. Willis, who is credited for changing the name "Butter Hill" to "Storm King Mountain", is also credited for the change to the name "Moodna".

"Cornwall, 200 years" 1976
Cornwall public library

Salisbury Mills-1906-1909- The Erie's 3,200 foot long Moodna Viaduct is constructed, the last link in the Erie's new low grade freight cutoff. Later to be renamed the Graham Line in honor of Joseph M. Graham, the Erie's Vice President of engineering who designed the cutoff.[2]

---

[2] *From the author's book "Erie Railroad-Schunemunk and shortcuts"*

The Viaduct is reflected in the waters of Moodna Creek

Author's photo

From the Cornwall Local, 1931:

"Sixty years ago"

"....The prediction of John Jacob Astor many years ago that Cornwall would someday be a populous and prosperous town is likely to be realized. Its location decides the place and time. The unbroken cliffs of the Palisades and the barriers of the Highlands barring access to the river, at difficult points gives Cornwall the first feasible site for a town above Jersey City on the west bank.

It is also the first having a rich and populous country in its rear. It is upon the banks of a tidewater river, deep enough to float the largest vessel that rides upon the sea, opening it to the commerce of the world. It is not only above the mountain range and on the unobstructed line of transcontinental commerce between the great west and New England and at the gateway of the highlands, where nature has indicated the bridging of the Hudson, binding with iron bands the vast railway system of the west with that of the east.; but to these advantages may be added the valley of the Moodna upon the north, forging a natural outlet to tidewater for the Erie Railway, making Cornwall one of its river termini, giving to it all the advantages of a trunk line of railroad to the interior and to the west, bringing the products of a vast traffic to the margin of the river here.

The Moodna flats by filling are admirably adapted to the shipment of coal, lumber, stone and other heavy objects. These are some of the advantages that inspire hope in the future growth and prosperity of Cornwall."

Leaving the business district of Cornwall (Canterbury) going south, Lewis Beach describes the power of Idlewild Brook (as it flows towards the mouth of the Moodna) and the stone bridge which to this day, defies the powers of the waters coming out of the mountains:

"As you emerge from Canterbury on the south, you cross the stone bridge. Through the double arch-ways of this antique structure, flow the waters of Idlewild Brook.; at times gently, at others, madly-wildly. The stone bridge, with its rude simplicity and rough but substantial masonry, always attracts favorable comments from strangers. It was built many, many years ago, fashioned after no particular model, and without aim at architectural beauty. Yet the graceful curve to the walls; and with the winding sweep of by which it is guarded on either side, give it a rustic charm which no amount of design or art could have ever affected. The midsummer visitor, who sees the dark and sluggish pool of water beneath the arches, can have but faint conception of the angry torrent into which that pool is often swollen during the spring and summer freshets. The various streams and rivulets of the mountain-side, unite in bringing watery tribute to this spot, and, after a heavy rain, the relentless flood beats for passage through the now dwarfed arch-ways, and, failing to find it, rushes impetuously to the south, completely submerging the road-bed. Full many a time, the old stone bridge has withstood the onslaught of the waters; yet there it stands-immovable-intact-the victor of a hundred battles."

O&W's Parlor Car "Moodna" at Middletown in the 1930's
The O&W named its parlor car fleet for the creeks
and rivers along the line.
O&WRHS

Climbing the grade out of Cornwall, and paralleling
Moodna all the way into Firthcliffe,

Train No.1 is just past the recently completed Rt. 9W Bridge
8/30/41 (Saturday)
225 and her sisters had already been pulled wartime traffic once in their career. Sadly, only four months remain before they will be called on to do it again.

The O&W once had a spur down to the Hercules Paper Mill
Just ahead of train 1, as well as small storage yard;
Back in the heyday of the coal business

Ed Crist albums/author's collection

Excerpts from the Cornwall Reflector

August 18 1886

"The N.Y.L.O. and Western Railroad* has secured, with two or three exceptions, the rights of way from Fair Oaks to Cornwall Landing and all except through one piece of property, to its Weehawken terminus, opposite New York, and we have been assured that the whole road will be put under contract within a month, at the farthest. It was officially announced in New York City last week that the road would be pushed forward at most rapid rate. It was also announced that estimates and plans have been prepared for a reduction of the grades on the existing road and in fifteen months the company will have in operation a line of 425 miles of first class railroad, including branches, from tidewater to Oswego, of which Low is to be President and Walter Katte, formerly chief engineer of the elevated railways, has been appointed Chief Engineer for the construction of the railroad and all the improvements

The NYLO &W Railroad Company has spent a large sum of money this season in bettering the road between Middletown and Lake Ontario. About 200.000 new ties and 2.000 tons of new steel rails have been laid on the line and sixty miles of new road ballasted. The woodwork on all the great iron structures has been renewed and a number of trestles. Some 150 cars have been rebuilt at the shops and al the engines have been put in first class shape. All the damaged cars have been worked up and the wrecked rolling stock at the different shops has about disappeared.

The chief engineer' plans were approved and it was arranged "to let" the work on the whole line immediately. Forty-five thousand shares, small certificates, are prepared for transmission to London, Paris, Frankfort and Amsterdam. "

The name "New York Lake Ontario and Western Railroad would be changed, dropping "Lake" not too far into the new venture.

Ghosts of Firthcliffe-Firth office building

Next page: T.F Firth & Sons, Bailiff Bridge West Yorkshire (UK)
Online search

"Show me a Scotchman who doesn't love the thistle.
Show me an Englishman who doesn't love the Rose.
Show me a true hearted son of old Erin who doesn't love the land where the Shamrock grows.
Show me a Weaver who doesn't love his shuttle;
Show me a working man who doesn't love his tools;
Show me the true-hearted son of endeavor who doesn't love the spot where the Firth name rules."
F. J. Collier, 1903

Chapter One:
The early years

FIRTH MILL, Firthcliffe, N. Y.

THE MILL BELL

The year of 1812 brought an important industrial development to the bank of Moodna Creek.

Henry Townsend built the Cornwall Cotton factory which was to become the beginning of future important growth. The company served the purpose of the community for many years, was rebuilt in 1849, and the latter half of the nineteenth century was taken over by Joseph Broadhead.

At this time located in its bed atop the stair tower of the original four story building was the "village bell" whose voice summoned people to work and told of the time of quitting. In addition, bell gave the call for Firefighters to bestir themselves. It served the community well for a long time; however, progress brought about further changes.

Above from Cornwall Historical Society
The tale from Sam Docherty, below, picks up the story from there:

Perched on top of our Spinning Mill is an old bell that for many years served as a signal for the employees of the old cotton and blanket mill back in 1840 and perhaps earlier than that date. Known to them as Townsend's Mill and later Broadhead's Mill, the bell occupied a place on the roof of the stairway on the building that we know of as lower carding, Spinning and Twisting. It is quite possible that the bell is much older than this date and would indicate and we can be excused for considering it as one of the few remaining links with the past- perhaps as far back as 1776.

What could be more fitting, I thought, than to bring the bell back to its former home so that it might continue to fill a place of responsibility in our community by ringing the "all clear" for our air-raid drills. It was only a step from this thought to a nostalgic wish that I might speak for the bell and tell its story to the new generations that now live in our community; and so follows:

THE SAGA OF THE BELL

I had heard of the bell quite by accident, and, with the thought that it might come in useful as an "all clear" signal, I stored the information in my mind for future investigation. A few days later I took an hour or so from my duties to call on Mrs. Newton Staples, who I was informed, had the bell stored on her property. Turning off the Route 9W By-pass at Moodna I followed the road up the little valley to the Staple's homestead. On inquiring for Mrs. Staples, I was informed that she was out in the fields busy with her farm work. As I sauntered across the upturned earth to meet her, the lines of Gray's "Eulogy" came to mind and seemed to fit the quiet peaceful spot as if made for it.

"The curfew tolls the knell of parting day, the lowing
herd winds slowly to the lea,
The ploughman homeward plods his weary way and
and leaves the world to darkness and to me"

I was jolted out of my dreaming with a cheery good afternoon from Mrs. Staples, and when I introduced myself she smiled and replied "Of course I remember you. Can I be of some assistance?"
I related my meager information concerning the bell that I was looking for and the use it might be to the community. The story she told me of her knowledge of the bell is here set forth in her own words.
"It was in 1908 that the bell came to our little village. We had built a church in Moodna and what a proud day that was when it was finished. However, it lacked one thing-a bell. We discussed this problem at great length and finally, my brother, Charles Wands, thought of the bell on the Firth Mill at Firthcliffe. On advice our minister, Gordon Whiteman, we appointed a committee to seethe officials of the Firth Carpet

Company. Our request was not only granted but in addition the old bell was removed from the position it had held for so many years and delivered to us at the church by Joe Van Duzer, Tom Martin and Chauncey Brown.

"I cannot tell you how much peace and comfort that bell has brought to our little community", she continued. "Its mellow tones seem to cloak the valley with a religious dignity that could not help but turn our thoughts away from the harsh things of life to the loftier, comforting feeling of Faith and Hope in our creator".

"But the time came when the bell no longer rang for Easter and Christmas. With our people moving out of the valley it was impossible to maintain our church and the bell was taken down and stored at my place. Many times I have sat here and pondered on it's history wondered just how old it was".

At this point a call from one of her grandchildren broke our pleasant half hour of reminiscing and Mrs. Staples left to attend to some special chore that only grandmothers can do.

I sat down by the old bell and lit a cigarette, a curious urge came over me to examine it for some strange mark or inscription that might be a guide to its age. Looking over the outside of it, I could find nothing to help me. Picking up a heavy bar, I pried up the edge of the bell about six inches and saw something that almost made me swallow my half smoked cigarette. There, before my eyes, two "little people" crawled out from under the bell and dusting their gaudy clothes, perched themselves on the outside lip. I held my breath lest I blew them away, (they were only about five inches high). While trying to frantically to adjust myself to this dreamlike trance I seemed to be in, a sweet musical note broke the stillness of the air as the "little man" stood up, bowed and said "I am Ding", followed by the little lady who curtsied, so low I could see the back of her Quaker bonnet as she echoed "I am Dong".

Scarcely breathing I replied "I am pleased to meet you." The tones of my voice seeming to crash on my eardrums with a discordant sound. I had barely time to note how they were dressed-She in a tight-waisted dress with billowy skirt and Quaker bonnet, so beautifully matched in the colors as to beggar description – He in knee britches buckled shoes with a curious little coat to match."

Again the silvery tones of Ding reached my ears as he asked "have you come to take us away from the valley?" "No" I replied, "I just want to take you back up the valley a little ways, back to your old home where you spent so many years of your life." As I glanced at Dong a crystal like tear, so small you could hardly see it, trickled down her worn cheek and I discreetly lowered my eyes to save her the embarrassment of my presence. Giving her time to recover I continued "Won't you tell me something about yourselves?"

Ding, standing up and stretching up his full five inches, exclaimed "Well, sir.---" but before he could start, Dong, with a shrewish look in her eyes, gently silenced him with a firm but courteous "Now Ding, you know my name is Dong. and through all our years together I have always had the last word. Sitting down on the edge of the bell (at my request) the amazing story is just as it fell from her trembling lips.

"It's been so many years since we last came here that I can scarcely remember. Seems to me it was about 1750, but goodness me I have never had a head for figures. First place I remember was Stony Point, all of us bells came from around that place. Will I ever forget the day Mr. Townsend came and brought us up to Montana (it was changed later to Firthcliffe, called after some Lord or Duke over in England) What a ride that was, two days it took with as fine an ox team as ever drew a cart. Then we were put in place on the mill, my we could see for miles around, and life from there was spent in useful work."

We have been together many years, Ding and I.", and putting her arm around his waist to keep him from falling (he was asleep by this time) "and now we can turn again to some useful work in our old age."

"Perhaps, she continued, "we can ring out our message at Eastertime and Christmastime, to herald joy and peace to all who hear us." "Yes, I replied, your fondest hopes and dreams are about to be realized because your task will be to ring the "all clear"; that is an honor reserved for those whose lives have been as useful as inspiring as yours. I am sure it must thrill you to know that your resonant, mellow tones from now on will tell our people that danger is over and they can continue to go about their work without fear. I know that the sound of your voice will be welcomed to all who hear it."

Just then the weird shriek of a train whistle shattered the stillness of the air and in my momentary distraction as I turned to address the "little people" they had disappeared as if they never existed. I wouldn't dare tell this to anyone, so I am setting this episode down for just my own satisfaction.

So I will file this away to gather dust and be hidden from the eyes of those who would scoff. But, if they had seen that sweet little old lady, Dong, they would stay and pray that she might someday ring out the "all clear" that would once again bring peace and contentment to our community and nation."

Mr. and Mrs. John Staples

Firth employees, circa turn of the century
One of those rare gems when a turn of the century photo has almost all of the names available
Cornwall Historical Society

1st row, L.toR: Frank Sampacks, John Heniher, Ted Redfern, William Schofield, John Schofield, Harry Sutcliffe, Jim Schofield, George Horton, Thomas Chandler
Short row, 3 men on right: Fred Leach, Joe Connor, Jim Daldon
2nd row, L.toR.: John Thornton, Anthony Westover, George Shearer, Ben Schofield, Jim Halstead, Joe (Shine) Smith, ? Dobson, Joe Burns, Harry Halstead
3rd row, L.to R.: ? Babcock, Mike Holloran, Charles Knowles, Thos. Hansen, George Taylor, Bill Burll

From Marjorie Taylor, 8/94

Fred Booth

"Twenty four year old Clerk Fred Booth travelled on the S.S.Scythia from Liverpool to New York arriving there on 15th February 1884. He was "to superintend the plant of this company (Firth Carpet Company), then located in Philadelphia." It was in Philadelphia that 25-year-old Fred Booth married 23-year-old Lydia Hurst on 15th June 1885. Both were residents of Philadelphia and under the remarks column it says "At there [sic] Home". Later censuses would state that Lydia was also originally from England but no further information has been found."

Online search

Fred Booth, a later photo *Cornwall Local*

Family Name	Given Name or Names
BOOTH	FRED

Title and Location of Court
COMMON PLEAS COURT, NEW YORK COUNTY.

Date of Naturalization	Volume or Bundle No.	Page No.	Copy of Record No.
JUNE-19-1889	659	—	87

Address of Naturalized Person
CORNWALL ON HUDSON   N.Y.

Occupation	Birth Date or Age	Former Nationality
SUPT.		ENGLISH

Port of Arrival in the United States	Date of Arrival
	FEB-1884

Names, Addresses and Occupations of Witnesses To Naturalization
1. JAMES C. SMITH   240 E. 41 ST. N.Y.C
2.

STATE OF NEW YORK, City and County of New York, ss. I, Fred Booth, residing in No. Cornwall on Hudson, do solemnly swear that I will support the Constitution of the United States; and that I do absolutely and entirely renounce and abjure all allegiance and fidelity to every foreign prince, Potentate, State or sovereignty whatever, and particularly to the Queen of the United Kingdom of Great Britain and Ireland, of whom I was before a subject.

Fred Booth

Sworn in open Court, this 19 day of June 189_
CLERK.

Booth's immigration papers
Online search

(Above) Firth company house
In the early years of the 20th century a housing shortage for the growing number of employees made it a possibility that Firth was going to have to move parts of its operations elsewhere.
Cornwall Public Library

THE HOLLOW Firthcliffe, N. Y

Carding Machine

The invention of the Spinning Jenny and the Spinning Frame caused an increase in demand for cardings. In 1748 Lewis Paul invented a hand driven carding machine. The devise involved a card covered with slips of wire placed round a cylinder. Richard Arkwright made improvements in this machine and in 1775 took out a patent for a new Carding Engine. Arkwright's machine included a cylinder carding engine, incorporating a crank and comb mechanism. The comb moved up and down, removing the carded fibers from the doffing cylinder in a "continuous filmy fleece".

Drawing of Carding Machine

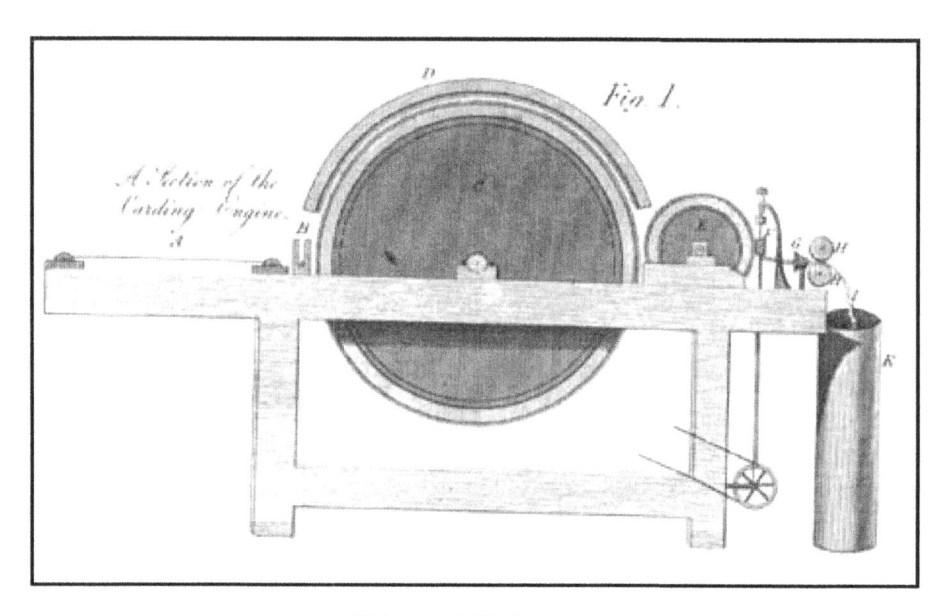

<u>Edward Baines</u>,

History of the Cotton Manufacture in Great Britain

(1935)

Lewis Paul's carding patent is dated 30th August, 1748. The machine had a horizontal cylinder, covered in its whole circumference with parallel rows of cards, with intervening spaces, and turned by a handle.

One of the first improvements made in the carding machine was the fixing of a perpetual revolting cloth, called a feeder, on which a given weight of cotton wool was spread, and, by which it was conveyed to the cylinder. This was invented in 1772, by John Lees, a Quaker, of Manchester.

When Arkwright took out his patent for the carding machine, he also included in it machines for drawing and roving. It consists in drawing out the carding by rollers, and then doubling and redoubling the slivers, which are called ends, so as to restore them to nearly the same substance as at first.

Illustration of carding, drawing and roving that appeared in Edward Baines' book History of Cotton Manufacture (1835)

The Carding Engine was not invented at once, nor by any particular individual, but was the result of a succession of improvements, made at various times, and by different persons. In this machine a wooden cylinder, covered with cards, turning on an horizontal axis, revolves immediately under a concave cover; the cover is also lined with cards, and the teeth of the cards on the cylinder and of those on the cover, are nearly in contact.

Originally, the cotton was spread upon the cylinder, and the cylinder by its revolutions carded the cotton against the teeth on the cover: the cotton was then taken off the cylinder by hand cards held against it. A great improvement was afterwards made by adding a second cylinder, which took the cotton off the first as fast as it was carded, and a roller, fluted longitudinally, and turning on a horizontal axis, pressed against this second cylinder and rubbed off the carded cotton in stripes.
Google search

Skein: bundle of yarn: a length of yarn or thread wound loosely and coiled together

In November of 1909 this article appeared in the Machinist's Monthly Journal

Contract Labor Law Violated
Late in November the Department of Commerce and Labor issued orders from Washington for the immediate deportation of several persons who had violated the contract labor law.
Fifty-three persons, cither contract laborers or dependents, who came to this country under an alleged unlawful arrangement with the Firth Carpet Company, located at Firthcliffe, N. Y., have been ordered to be returned to their homes in England and Scotland.
The cases of many others are under consideration, but no final disposition has been made of them. The Department of Justice has the prosecution of the Firth Carpet Company, for violation of the contract labor laws, under advisement.
It was charged in a report to the Department of Commerce and Labor last June that the Firth Carpet Company had violated the contract labor law. The department, in a statement, says that after examination of various employees of the concern, it was convinced that wholesale importations of laborers had been effected.
In the course of the examination some half dozen aliens arrived at New York, all destined to Firthcliffe. They were ordered to be deported. Subsequently, on the report of the investigating officers, eighty-eight persons were ordered arrested. They included contract laborers and their immediate families.
Firthcliffe is a small village in Orange County, New York. Practically the only industry is the Firth Carpet Company, employing six hundred men. The president and the principal owners are said to be Englishmen, who are identified with similar concerns in Great Britain. A large percentage of the employees of the concern are experienced tapestry workers, who have received their training in English and Scotch carpet mills. The department claims in its statement that the books of the company show that from 1902 to 1908 over $4,410 had been advanced to aliens to enable them to migrate to Firthcliffe.
Google Earth search

T.F Firth & Sons, Bailiff Bridge West Yorkshire (UK)

Online search

Firth mill workers, either of which could very well be my great-grandfather
George Kane

St. Patrick's Rock
Off Frost Lane

*(Now within the bounds of
Private property)*

Chapter Two:
Out and about...

1. Wm. Sutcliffe, 2. James Halstead, 3. Thomas Chandler, 4. John Halstead ?, 5. John Arnott, 6. Arthur Ogden, 7. Thomas Greenwood, 8. Ernest Smith, 9. John Chandler 10. Percy Doyle.

Photo courtesy of Jack Arnott

Eureka Hotel, later the Villa Pennisi, Cornwall Landing

In the days before the O&W took vacationers to the Catskill mountains, Cornwall was the place travelers came to by steamboat to escape the city summer heat.

Liberty station, Sullivan County

Otto Hillig[3] photo/Ed Crist albums/author's collection

This beautiful station was one of the hubs of the O&W's summer hotel business. Lines of carriages lined the street waiting to take travelers to hotels such as the legendary Grossinger's Hotel.

---

[3] Otto Hillig was born in Steinbruechen, Germany in 1874 and when sixteen years of age came to the United States as a poor German immigrant. He first worked as a street car conductor in Brooklyn, later as a bartender and still later as a laborer in a brewery in Ellenville. When about twenty-one years of age and virtually penniless, he moved into the Liberty area and while working on a farm near White Sulphur Springs supposedly found a photo magazine and decided to try his hand at photography. He went on to become the most famous photographer in Sullivan County and the owner of the best equipped studio between New York City and Buffalo. Said to have taken over 10,000 photos *Sullivan County Historical Society*

In the 1890's, these articles appeared in the Cornwall Reflector. While not all pertaining to Firthcliffe, they give a cross section of life at the turn of the century.

"The superb steam propeller Homer Ramsdell made her last Sunday morning trip from foot of Franklin Street New York City to her wharf in Newburgh in 3 hours and 11 minutes. This is the fastest propeller record ever made."

"The usual Saturday night dances were enjoyed by the guests at the Mountain House and the Elmer last week. That on the heights was a fancy dress ball and created a great deal of hilarity by the grotesqueness of many of the costumes."

"It is strange how few know how to dispose of the cup at the Cold Spring after drinking from it. Almost invariably it is placed upon the projection between the pipe and the trough. Here it is slobbered in by the horses that drink at the trough. The cup should be hung over the top of the hydrant. Here it is out of danger.

"Two New York City young ladies had sad experience in boating on Friday evening of last week. After a very pleasant row on the bay, as they were attempting to land at Clark's dock their escort permitted the boat to slip from under them and they were precipitated into the water. Captain Ruben Clark helped them to terra firma again."

"The St John's Church Ladies aid Society opened their fair for the benefit of the Town Clock fund, on Tuesday afternoon at 4 O'clock and continued it during Wednesday afternoon and evening, and notwithstanding the unfavorable weather it was successful as a display of taste and good management, and financially the receipts being $400. The chair was voted to the Rev. W.E. Snowden and the elegant quilt to Edward Mcullom. The clock is assured.

"Emslie Post* No. 546 G.A.R. have extended invitations to various posts in Orange and neighboring counties to be their guests during the reunion of the 124th Regiment in the village on September 6."
*Named for William Emslie, who died in the Civil War

The news was not always pleasant. Mr. John Mitchell of Meadowbrook farm was paid $150.00 for his young bull Frank's Viking that had been recently killed by the N.Y.O. & W. Railroad. And the body of an unidentified man was found floating in Orrs Mills pond. And two freight cars and their cargo were damaged in a "smashup" at Montana.

Here are some of the Events, both historic and tragic, that would occur in that first decade of the 20th century:

1901: Theodore Roosevelt becomes President after the tragic death of President William McKinley from an assassin's s bullet.

1902: Work begins in New York City on The Pennsylvania Railroad's colossal Pennsylvania station. The Pennsylvania Railroad inaugurates it's The Broadway Limited, the train that will become its signature train. While The New York Central Railroad inaugurates what will become its signature train-the Twentieth Century Limited, the beginning of a rivalry between these two trains that will last for six decades.

1903: The Wright brothers make the first successful airplane flight at Kitty Hawk. In New York City, work begins on the New York Central Railroad's Grand Central Terminal.

1904: The first subway line in New York City opens.
Work begins on the Panama Canal.

1906: Work begins on the steamship Lusitania. Her sinking by a German U Boat nine years later will accelerate America's entry into the First World War. The city of San Francisco is destroyed by an earthquake and subsequent fire.
1908: Henry Ford produces the first Model "T" automobile, the start of a transportation revolution that will change the world forever.

1909: Work begins on the steamship Titanic. Her tragic loss just three years later will change the rules for ship safety
Cornwall Local, 1901:

"From our regular correspondent"

Sidewalks in Firthcliffe are in a very poor condition at present.
Charley Wands is again able to take up employment in the Firth Carpet Company.
Ground has been broken for a new house which is to be erected for Mr. Samuel Crabtree.
The sale of the Broadhead property begins next Saturday afternoon at two o'clock sharp.
The Firth Carpet Company baseball team would be pleased to hear from other teams along the Hudson.
Sunday evening services began in the British-American rooms last Sunday evening. All are invited to attend.
Mr. Beaumont Sykes will deliver a lecture on "Trusts and their ultimate outcome" in the British-American hall, Saturday evening, May 4th, 1901. A good attendance is desired.

You "Auto" Be with us in Moutainville, N.Y.

"Outstanding in the minds of all the boys in attendance that year is "the big snow" of December 13th and 14th (1914)

Beginning with a light fall that Monday morning, the storm increased in severity to blizzard proportions and continued for more than thirty-six hours. At the end of that time there was no less than thirty-eight inches of snow. The weight of the snow caused the collapse of several old buildings, and made all roads impassable to ordinary traffic. Troop D was mustered into service however, and forty horsemen in columns of two, broke roads to the station and Orr's Mills in order that a much needed milk supply might be brought to the Academy

Cold and more snow continued through the winter until the total snowfall was more than ten feet. "Old grads" still recall the use of sleighs of all descriptions for the exodus at the time of Christmas vacation. The going was still so bad that many sleighs overturned, depositing cadets and luggage in small mountains of snow along the roadside"

New York Military Academy
"Shrapnel" 50th anniversary yearbook

5 Bede Terrace-early 1900's- built/owned by the Wardens, John Warden (1850-1945) was a weaver

Lynn McCarthy

Chapter Three:
The great flood of 1903

**TOWN OF CORNWALL
SWEPT BY FLOOD!**

Damages Sustained by the Firth Carpet Mills, the Feed Mills, Railroads and Brick Yards.

The Orrs Mills Bridge Gone!

State Road badly damaged and Moodna Paper Mills are Heavy Losers.

Above and on the following pages are the headline story for the for the Cornwall Local on October 15, 1903.

Firth Mill flooded, 1903
Cornwall Public Library

"The town of Cornwall and vicinity last week suffered the worst devastation by flood that it has perhaps, ever experienced. The rain of Wednesday night was followed Thursday morning by showers which settled into a steady downpour before noon. It continued through the night with increasing power and by Friday morning every brook was a raging torrent. Still the storm did not abate and not until Friday afternoon was there a cessation of the rainfall. The water continued to rise for several hours afterward, and the showers of Saturday, Sunday did not admit of the streams getting back into their proper channels entirely, even by that time.

In the meantime, Moodna Creek had been converted into a raging river, and it was this stream that caused the greatest damage in different parts of the town. The Firth Caret Mills, the town's largest employer, is damaged to the extent of $15,000 to $20,000 dollars. The large iron bridge at Orrs Mills, a part of the state road, was entirely demolished, and a gaping waste of angry waters with a broken dam above tells the story. The new State road, along the route known as the creek road to Mountainville, is so badly damaged that travel over it was hazardous for the fore part of the week. Most of the travel to and from Mountainville was by way of the hill road or Angola. Hedges brick yards are heavily damaged. All traffic on the O&W was suspended until Monday. The West Shore trestle was curved into the shape of a letter S and trains have been run only with the utmost care and very slowly.

The Erie Railroad, even on most of its main lines, was running no trains until the fore part of the week, and the Short Cut is not in shape yet for use. The Garvin Paper Mills at Moodna are heavily damaged, and their dam is broken. (Continues)

The Firth Carpet Mill

A large new wagon shed lately erected at a cost of $1000 was completely demolished. A fortunate incident in connection was when the roof fell in it held the wagons firmly and thus prevented further loss while other equipment was washed away. Every barrel and cask in the color shop, of which there were three to four hundred, was washed out against the machinery and piled in heaps of every description.

The roads in the mill were washed out in places to the depth of five or six feet. The bed of the creek is changed so that the water runs over the bank at the lower portion of the yards, instead of against the retaining wall, which is one satisfactory change in connection with the general wreck.

One hundred and fifty men were put to work cleaning up as soon as the waters subsided. Scores of tons of gravel, mud, have been removed from the buildings. The spinning equipment started up for the first time Monday morning, also a few of the setters and weavers, and at each day thereafter, has seen more department men at work so that Superintendent Booth expects that by next Monday morning the entire plant will be in full operation again. The mills are so well built that they have withstood the flood without damage.

Wm. Orr and Sons Mills

Two broken dams are the principal damage sustained by the feed mills of Wm Orr & Sons. The large dam above the bridge is out on one end, and this cannot be replaced until the new bridge abutment is built. The lower race dam was entirely washed away. That is being rebuilt now, and is thought it will be in shape to commence running the mill in about ten days. Wm. Orr & Sons estimate their loss at about $1,500. The firm will establish a temporary station at Firthcliffe, serving their customers on this side with coal and feed from there.

Ontario and Western railroad

The track over a sluice near Moodna washed away and has been replaced by a bridge. Trains were run over it again the fore part of the week. The long trestle at Ors Mills remains firm.

The washout was for a distance of 150 feet and was caused by a clogging of a catch basin, the outlet of which was a two foot tile pipe. The waters backed up until the embankment could hold them no longer. An engine which was stationed on the track to help hold it firm was run off just in the nick of time. The roadbed moved as a single body about four feet down before it broke away. When part way down the grade, the mass seem to divide, part going one way and part the other, which probably accounts for the houses directly in its path not being swept into the stream.

WEST SHORE RAILROAD-TWO MEN KILLED

The West Shore road sustained quite heavy damages at different points along its route. The long trestle just above Cornwall was moved about nine inches on its foundation and all the work and grading which has been done this past summer has been undone. A landslide occurred at Yellow Point, between Highland and Milton, which buried two men beneath tons of earth. The bodies were not yet recovered on Tuesday.

J.W. Cooper, of Milton, a section Foreman, and one of his men, were the unfortunate victims. Several others escaped only by jumping into the river and swimming to the shore. The tracks were covered for quite a distance.
At Haverstraw, the bridge was washed out, but was replaced in a day or two. The Erie and Susquehanna roads have been running trains over this route this past week, coming by way of Middletown, and using the West Shore tracks as far as New Durham. At the entrance to the Weehawken tunnel, a great amount of mud was washed down so that only one track was used the fore part of this week

THE HEDGES BRICK YARDS

Here again, was widespread damage done. The water of the Moodna, rushing down with flood debris, accumulated against the West Shore trestle and backed up over Hedges Brick Yards, ruining about a half a million bricks in the kilns, and many others in the yards themselves. It is impossible to yet for Mr. Hedges to estimate closely the loss, but it will reach several thousand dollars.

(Below) *Summary of the remainder of the story from the pages of the Cornwall Local from that disastrous time:*

Garvin Paper Mills in Cornwall received an estimated $20.000 in damages, the dam being broke in two places and the Carpenter and machine shops washed away. Arlington Paper Mill in Salisbury Mills received equal damage and several houses along the Moodna were either moved from their foundations or washed away completely. Several families barely escaped with their lives while the West Shore Railroad lost two men.

Firth Carpet, note water up to windowsill
Cornwall Public Library

Disaster was to strike again in 1955, as chronicled in the Cornwall Local:

August 25th: The lower part of the spillway gate at Firth Carpet Company dam across Moodna Creek was struck by a log or other large object at 7 P.M. on Friday, renting a large hole and allowing a the raging waters of the swollen creek to pour into the raceway, flooding the lower portion of the mill. Inundated were the weave shop, which bore the brunt of the huge crest of flood water, the machine shop, store room yarn storage blending department and dye house. Water in some of the buildings was over three feet deep.

Russell Matthews, general manager of this large carpet manufacturing plant, which employees hundreds of men and women from around the area, stated on Monday that the damage was not as heavy as anticipated. Adding it would be sometime before the full extent of the damage could be determined.

During the height of the flood on Friday employees had placed sand bags around the gate for added protection. The flood waters had dropped one foot and it was felt that danger had passed when the break occurred in the spillway gate.

As soon as it was generally known the gate had been stove in between 400 and 500 hundred employees instantaneously flocked to the plant to assist in manner of ways to save what material and equipment they could.

Damage to a large number of rugs and other materials in the finishing department was averted by employees sandbagging the doorways to prevent the angry waters from rushing into the room.

When the gate broke Walter Dickinson, a guard on duty, cut the power on the 14.000 volt power line to the mill, eliminating the possibility and any employees working the night shift from being electrocuted.

On Monday afternoon Mr. Matthews announced that 80 percent of the plant was back in production and the entire mill would be in full production by the end of the week.

Despite rumors that the valuable looms in the weave shop were ruined, Mr. Matthews said they are still useable and are now being put back in shape.

Crews worked all day Saturday cleaning up debris left by the flood. When the gate broke, plant maintenance men in charge of Roger Williams, rushed to the scene of the break and by midnight had diverted the water to the creek through a large ditch dug with high pressure fire hoses and picks and shovels and the water started to recede in the lower part of the mill. At the same time a "beaver dam" of sand bags and large planks was constructed where the raceway entered the mill. Since then, maintenance men have strengthened the spillway gate and the temporary dam on the raceway.

It is proposed that the gate be eliminated and a solid masonry wall built in its place, with a large pipe regulated by a small gate placed in the wall.

Mr. Matthews pointed out that the raceway cannot be eliminated as the water must be stored there for use in carpet making operation. The village cannot supply sufficient water to meet the needs of the mill.

Ghosts of Firthcliffe: Stairwell, Firth Carpet

One of the buildings that was lost in the 2012 fire

Chapter Four:
Firthcliffe (Montana) Station, and the "tunnel"

"O. & W." R. R. Station, Firthcliffe, N. Y

All the stations on the O&W between Cornwall and Middletown were built out of a similar, but never exact, pattern: All two story wood frame buildings with living quarters for the Station Agent upstairs.

For a comparison on the following page, I offer these pictures of the now vanished Mechanicstown station, and Meadowbrook station on page 70, and pages 86-87

Mechanicstown station, lost to a fire in 2018,
the last surviving O&W "sister"

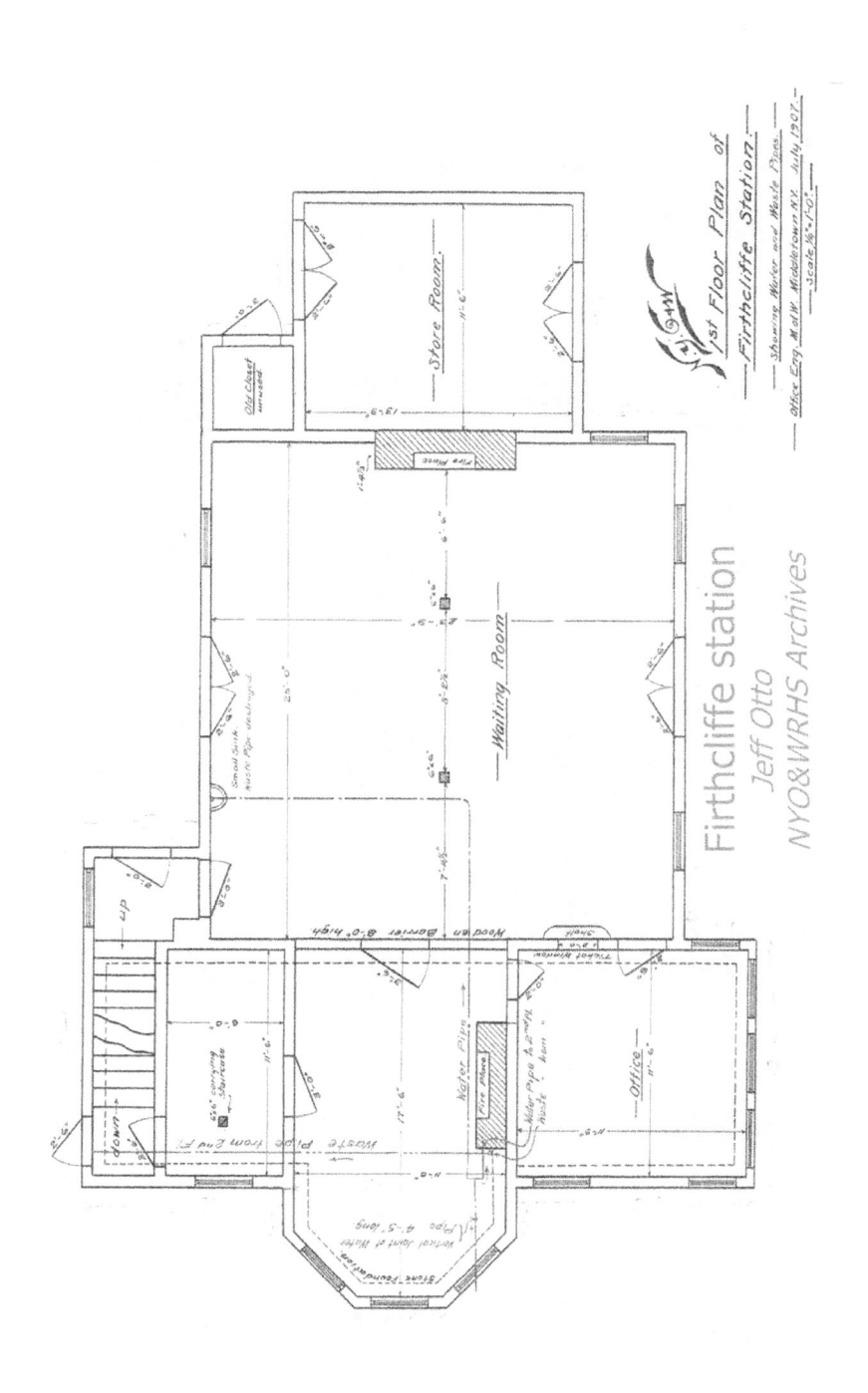

Similar stations can be found along the West Shore Railroad, since they were all built during the short lived West Shore/O&W years. But Firthcliffe's design is unique in that it is the only station between Cornwall and Middletown to receive a spire, Queen Anne-style windows and a bay.

In the end of the gable over the double windows the name MONTANA was carved into the side of the station, the original name of Firthcliffe before the carpet company moved in. The freight cars to the left would have been on the siding for the coal bin.

1909 O&WRHS collection

In the picture below, the fresh concrete ahead and to the left of the station platform is the new concrete underpass for Mill Street, built in 1910. The pipe railing in the background runs along the top of the underpass wall. From 1910 until the underpass was demolished in the early 1960s, drivers going through the underpass had to go through the hairpin "S" turn under the railroad tracks. Slowing down and honking the horn for drivers you couldn't see coming the other way was a bane for drivers for half a century, then a fond memory after. In the picture on the next page, work is about to begin on the overpass, as evidenced by the work train and materials by the tracks.

Both pictures, O&WRHS collection

The girl on the right could very well be one of my grandfather's sisters-He had five of them!

Firthcliffe was not the only underpass to receive this torturous turn. One is still in use on the former Erie Graham line in Highland Mills and there were others. The reasoning behind the hairpin, as the story goes, was to discourage the building of a trolley line. Trolleys were still the only real competition to the railroads in the first decade of the 20th century. *

See connecting story starting on page 78

(Top) digging the underpass
(Bottom) Work train at Firthcliffe, 1909, very likely
part of the same work detail in the picture on page 70.
Both O&WRHS collection

(Top) Postcard *Cornwall Public Library*

In 1886 confusion with Cornwall on
Hudson's incorporation as a village
led to the events in the following article:

"Under the present management of the West Shore, The Ontario and Western Railroad has no longer a depot at this landing, and in order to get a share of the Cornwall business has been obliged to utilize the Montana station and call it Cornwall Village. I think they can do better still by building a station on the Newburgh Road beyond the Glen Ridge Hotel and call it simply Cornwall, and if necessary, run a free stage to Canterbury and if advisable, through the Roe Avenue to the Library Hall, and as their trains will all run express (Not being permitted to stop nowhere after leaving Cornwall ,and only permitted to stop everywhere after leaving Cornwall, and only permitted to drop northern passengers there , those for the West Shore Road) They can land passengers to New York in less time than the West Shore Road.

I understand there is a movement on foot to annul the charter of incorporation. I do not propose to take any part in this movement. The permanent residents of Cornwall can now tell after a year's experience whether they want it or not and will no doubt act accordingly. But I am ready to do all I can to have the people go back to their own proper name of Cornwall on Hudson, and do away with the confusion of names is now puzzling so many.

Yours Truly, Cornwall Proper March 13, 1886"

THE INTERVALE TRACTION COMPANY

Further particulars about the new enterprise- Route-Stockholders

According to the articles of certificate of the incorporation of the Intervale Traction Company, the road will be a surface railroad and will be operated by electricity and operated by some motive power other than steam. It will be built and operated from the city of Newburgh to the village of Goshen, which place will be its terminal and the length will be twenty-eight miles. It will be located entirely within the county of Orange. The amount of capital stock is $300,000, divided into three thousand shares.

The route of the railway in detail as follows:

Beginning at Goshen, at the end of the tracks of the Middletown and Goshen Electric R.R., and running to Canal Street to Church Street; thence along Church Street and across Main Street to James Street; on James to Green; along Erie R.R. tracks; along same to South Street; thence to along Chester Avenue to a point south of the Erie R.R. crossing; thence along Florida Road to Chester and Goshen Road; thence along the same to Joseph Durland's store; thence down Main Street, Chester, to the road leading to Greycourt; thence to Greycourt on the same; then through private property to a point near Brook's Bridge on highway leading from Chester to Washingtonville; thence along highway to Main Street, Washingtonville; thence to through Main Street to corporate line; thence along highway continuation of said street to Phillips Hill; through private property around Phillips Hill to same highway; thence along highway through the village of Salisbury Mills; thence through private property to Vails Gate Station on the highway leading from Salisbury Mills to Newburgh; thence along highway to junction of said road and road leading from Knox's Headquarters to Cornwall; thence through private property to highway leading from Cornwall to Newburgh to the city line; thence along the same to Marvel Shipyard; thence through private property to Front Street; then on Front Street to a point intersecting with track of the Newburgh Electric R.R.; thence such streets as permissible may hereafter be granted by the City of Newburgh to construct such a railroad.

Each of the gentlemen named except one has subscribed for nineteen shares of stock for the corporation: Louis W. Stotesbury, 41 Park Row, New York City; William P. Lockwood, Washington, D.C.; Henry A. Pressey, Washington, D.C.; W Johnston McKay, Newburgh; Henry M. Finch, Washingtonville; Graham Witschief, J.A P. Ramsdell, H.P. Odell, Newburgh; Hector Moffat, Washingtonville; Fredrick W. Seward, Goshen; Alfred C. Greening, New York City; Charles A. Burt, New York City; Edward R. Emerson, Washingtonville; Charles D. Hobbs, New York City; Charles W. Griffith, New York City; B.J. Richards, Mechanicsville; Mr. Greening has subscribed for fifteen shares.

          Newburgh Journal

Even without further research, the outcome of this grand plan was obvious. The Erie would have fought it from the start. And the coming of the auto age would have been the *coup de grace.*

    (Above) *From the pages of the Cornwall Local*
                April 25th, 1901

Drivers traveling through Salisbury Mills today pass under the Erie's Graham line (today's Metro North line) on Rt.94 via a high steel bridge with the fading Erie Name on it. But from the time the Gram line was opened in 19o9 until the 1930's drivers had to negotiate a hairpin turn through a concrete tunnel under the tracks to the right of the present underpass. This would have discouraged for all time the traction railroad in the story above, which would have run in direct competition with passenger service on the Erie's

Newburgh to Greycourt branch. The tunnel survives today (2010) at the end of a private driveway

The treacherous "S" turn in the Firthcliffe underpass was not long after opening to gain its infamous reputation, as the first of the two following articles attest to in the *Newburgh Daily News,* both from October, 1910:

Firthcliffe Oct. 10, 1910:

"A bad accident occurred at the Firthcliffe under grade crossing Saturday afternoon about 3 o'clock, when Mason & Hanger's automobile ran into a horse and wagon driven by William Wilson of Orr's Mills.

There is a right angle turn at this point, which makes it impossible for those coming from the opposite direction to see each other for any considerable distance.

Mr. Wilson could not see the automobile approaching and when it came suddenly upon him from around the turn the horse was so badly frightened that he bolted and threw Mr. Wilson, who is along in years, out of the wagon. Mr. Wilson sustained a fracture of ribs and a broken thumb. His horse was caught near the ball grounds."

Newburgh Public Library

SALT WATER EXCURSION
To
NEW YORK CITY AND RETURN
Sunday, September 18, 1927

Via

NEW YORK ONTARIO & WESTERN RAILWAY

Train leaves Firthcliffe at 9:15 A.M. Eastern Standard Time

Round trip fare: $2:00

For further particulars apply to Agent or address

G.L. Robinson G.P.A. W.M. Tiel, D.P.A.
New York City Middletown, N.Y.

Cornwall Local/Cornwall Public Library

(Below and next page) Credit to Alan Furler

Below and next page: NYO&W Train No. 9 with Class Y-1 "Mountain" No. 408 nearing Firthcliffe on 3-23-1946. *The original 4x5" negative is in the Donald W. Furler Collection of the Center for Railroad Photography & Art.*

The O&W's "Mountain" locomotives came to the railroad in the 1920's. Sister 402 would make the last steam run on the Ontario and Western on July 21st, 1948.

The view of the station in the distance is the same as on the next page, in a later photo.

#9, having stopped to waiting for clearance to proceed, now has the go-ahead, and the 408 is kicking up a cloud of steam and smoke as she digs in her heels for the uphill run to Little Britain, the crest of the climb out of Cornwall.

The station in the later years, with what would appear
to be a Desoto under the canopy-any car buffs out there?
*The name "Montana", carved into the siding, can just be made
out above the baggage room windows.*

Few things made by the human hand more noble than the railroad station
Day and night, sun and storm, there she stands, ready to greet the next weary soul who steps onto the platform
She has seen its share of hellos, and her share of goodbyes
In her youth the paint was bright, the roof ready to stand off the storms thrown her way
In old age the paint has faded, the roof looks weary, and the old building a curiosity to kids who explore musty rooms with faded wallpaper, and hatchways to the attic steeple
When the trains are gone, the rails rusty, the old station will have her memories to keep her company
She will not lament the end of her usefulness and her life
She looks forward to rejoining the young soldiers to whom she said goodbye to and that never returned.
They will swap stories of being young again
Of watching the big steam engines roll through that once shook her gables, smoke and steam filling the air
And the engineer who waved to station and child as he rolled by
The red caboose on the last coupler as it disappeared around the curve with a wave from a hand in the cupola
It all happened right here, under the watchful eye of a noble building called a railroad station

Bob McCue

Above and next page: Mechanicstown station

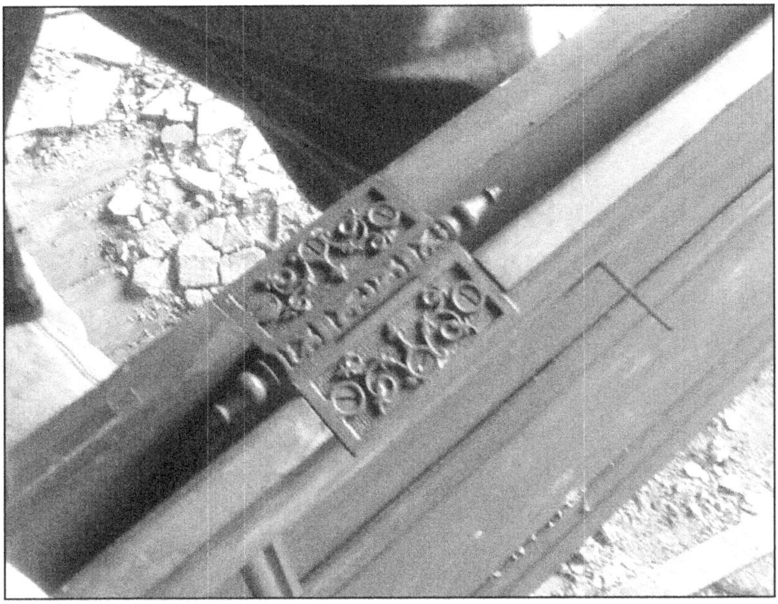

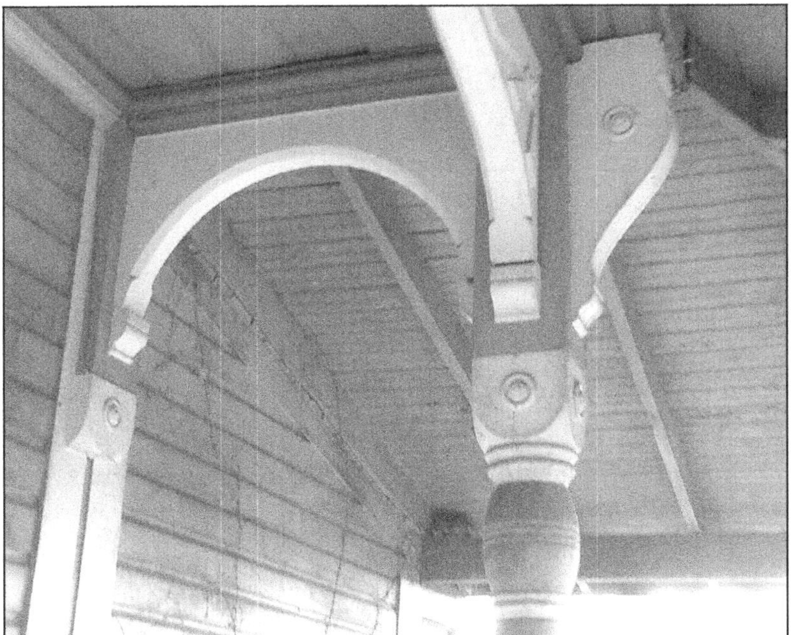

Firthcliffe, The last years
O&WRHS

The station met its fiery end in the early hours of September 18, 1963. Fire Chief Joe Ward said that the alarm was sounded at 5A.M. and called in by Mrs. Ellen Keator. When the fire department arrived the plywood was already falling off the windows. Several fires had been put out in the building in the past months. This time the destruction was total.

John Stagliano, who grew up in Firthcliffe (another "Firthco Rat" as they called themselves with affection) would recall the inside of the station in those final years:

"All the doors were wide open. The place was kind of spooky and hesitantly we went in, in the waiting room the wood benches sat solemnly covered in dust. Up on the oak walls were still World War Two posters saying things like "loose lips sink ships" and "Uncle Sam needs you" and "V for Victory", there were others with scenes of train's from a by-gone era. The office doors were open, revealing hundreds of RR timetables and many other volumes of paper.
I sensed the overwhelming presence of history, all around me, and it was enticing to say the least!
I didn't notice any big clock or telegraph equipment, and I had the suspicion that others had visited the station previously, and had taken many items with them."

(Below and next page) Demolishing the overpass 1966

Edward Smith, who grew up in Firthcliffe, recalls that in the tunnel going down to the Firth mill there was only one light bulb for the entire thing, probably a 100 watt and that was it. Remembering the tunnel, he can vividly recall what somebody wrote on the side of the tunnel wall...."Get my million dollar baby out of this ten cent hole"! At the train station there was a side car that you got on and pumped to ride the tracks.

Filling in the underpass, the burned out remains of the station are in the background.
Cornwall Local, Cornwall Historical Society

"Fire guts Coal pocket Sunday"
From the Cornwall Local, Sept., 1958

"A fire, apparently caused by spontaneous combustion, gutted the roof of the Firth Carpet Company coal pocket, adjacent to the Ontario and Western Railroad tracks on Sunday evening. The alarm went up at 7 p.m. and when the Highland Engine Company arrived in Command of Chief Arthur DeVoe, the building, which has stone sides and a wooden roof, was a mass of flames. For one and a half hours the Highland firemen, assisted by Storm King Engine Company, fought the flames and were able to save a huge pile of coal on the ground near the pocket. There was very little coal in the structure at the time it burned. Three two and a half (inch) lines were used as well as water from the Storm King engine's booster tank."

The coal shed burned On Sept. 18 of 1958, five years almost to the day that the Firthcliffe station would burn. By coincidence, it had also been 6 years to the day that the O&W coal docks at Cornwall had burned, burning on September 18 of 1952 in a massive fire that could be seen by all accounts three miles inland. Ed Crist, longtime Firthcliffe resident, recalls the tin roof melting from the intense heat. *Cornwall Local/Cornwall Public Library*

> (Next three pages) Ghosts of Firthcliffe: The remains of the coal shed that once served Firthcliffe and the Carpet Company. Just up and across from the station. Lines of coal cars were once switched out here to be emptied into the bin below. The abandoned machinery lay in place into the 1980's

Ruins of coal bin

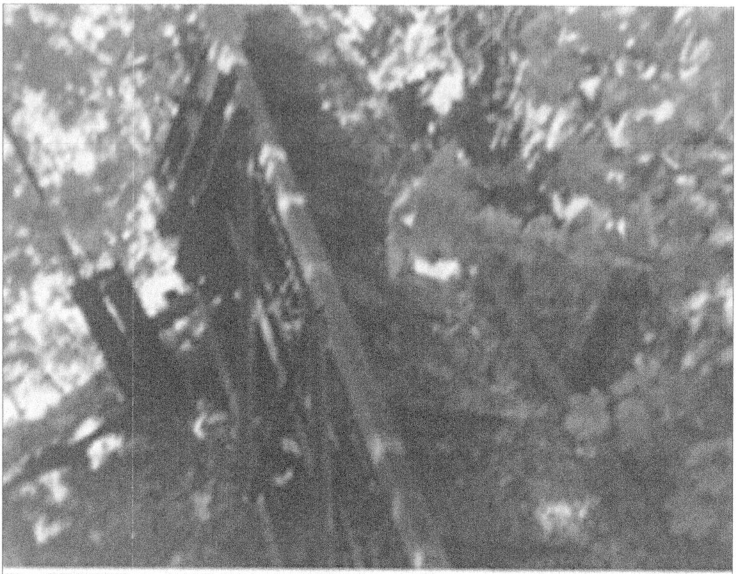

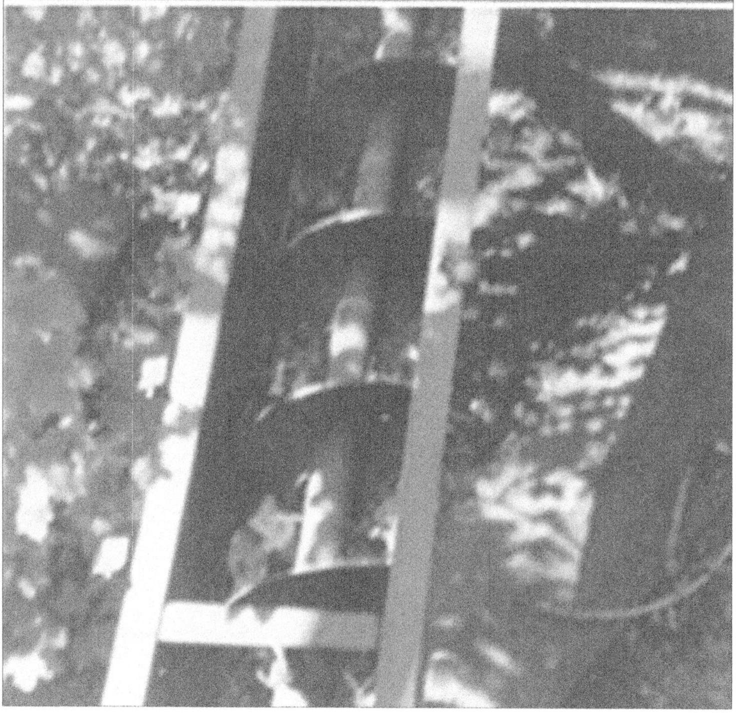

Ghosts of Firthcliffe: (Top) railing along top of underpass
(Bottom)
Station ruins, with the bay window in the center

"Firth Villa" Then and now
Up until about 1920, Residence of the Firth family when they were in Cornwall

Chapter Five:
Firthcliffe Clubhouse

Firth Club House

On the following pages, is the full story of the opening of the opening of the Firthcliffe club as it appeared in the Cornwall Local on Thursday, December 10, 1903:

Club House opening
The Firth Carpet Company's
Princely Gift to its employees
Formally opened. Mr. A .F. Firth,
Vice President of the Company,
Presents and entertains by interesting Speech-Banquet and Dance.

The Furnishings, Etc.

"Monday evening, December 7, 1903, has made itself memorable to a goodly number of people, including the employees of the Firth Carpet Mills and a very pleasant company of invited guests. The occasion was the formal opening of the Firthcliffe Club's new building, presented by the Firth Carpet Company to its employees.

Mr. Algernon F. Firth, of Lightcliffe, near Halifax, England, vice President of the Firth Carpet Company, arrived in New York on Thursday, November 19th, by the steamer Teutonic, for the purpose of attending the opening, and his presence was the final element completing the pleasure of the event.

The building, of which, full description is given further on, was ablaze with light early in the evening, and by the hour scheduled for the exercises, eight o'clock, the rooms were thronged with a happy, social gathering, all set upon having a good time and helping others to do the same. And we thought (as we always do when we have the pleasure of attending any social event in Firthcliffe) that if the warm hearted, genial friendliness of the people of the people there is a characteristic of English in general at home, surely "Merrie England" is no misnomer.

The company gradually seated themselves in the assembly room on the second floor, where an abundance of chairs were provided, in readiness for the addresses of the evening. At one end of the room, the stage was handsomely furnished with elegant rugs of the company's own manufacture, and as a background, the stars and stripes and the union jack met in friendly embrace. A large portrait of the venerable president of the company, Mr. Thomas F. Firth, of Hockmonwike, England, was placed over the front of the stage, and a piano, chairs and palms completed the perspective.

Soon the following gentlemen took seats upon the stage: Mr. Algernon Firth, whose appearance was heralded with applause, and who presided as chairman; Mr. Fred Booth, Superintendent and Secretary of the Firth Carpet Company; Mr. Bennett H. Tobey of New York, selling Agent and Treasurer for the company; Mr. Fredrick J. Collier, of Hudson, N.Y., attorney for the company and also a director; Mr. James Aspinall, building manager for the company whose direction for the new building had been directed; and the Hon. John Orr of Orrs Mills, representative from this district to the capitol at Albany.

Mr. Firth first called upon Superintendent Booth, who extended a hearty welcome to the guests and spoke appropriately and effectively of the gratification felt upon completion and opening of the new edifice, and expressed the common pleasure of all in having Mr. Firth with us again. Mr. Booth also read letters of regret at their liability to be present from Governor O'Dell, the Hon. Thomas W. Bradley and the Rev. Dr. Lyman Abbot.

Mr. Firth then gave a most interesting talk. He first warmly seconded Mr. Booth's words of welcome, and spoke of the pleasure it was to be again among the people of Firthcliffe, many of whom he remembers as grown people when he was a boy, and still others of whom were youths with him, and have reached middle life with him. He desired especially to express the gratification they all felt regarding Mr. Booth's strength, and trusted that in his new home and improved surroundings, he might still further gain in health.

Mr. Firth then gave a brief historical sketch of the mills in Firthcliffe, which were established about eighteen years ago, not without considerable misgivings as to the outcome. The location has, however, proved to be all that could be desired, and the mills have grown to be a prosperous and stable institution. During all those years, short timer work has been unknown, the products being on a high grade and selling readily.

At the panic time of 1893, the Firth Carpet Mills only closed down some four to five weeks while most of the mills in the country were closed six months or more.

The ability to furnish steady work its employees has been a matter of much gratification to the management of the Firth Mills, and has been a fruitful source of strength to its employees. The mills have had their share of the phenomenal prosperity that which the country has enjoyed for a few years back. There has been a large demand for their goods and they have brought good prices. Wages at the Firth Mills have never been so good, and everyone has had a chance to lay a little by for the times when not so favorable, which are to come sometime. Right here Mr. Firth wish to emphatically advise all to save a portion of their wages for a rainy day. It is a matter of prudence and wise foresight to do so, and hoped all would avail themselves of the opportunity thus afforded in these years of prosperity.

Regarding the new building for the Firthcliffe club, Mr. Firth wished to express his pleasure in furnishing a place for the social enjoyment of the employees and their relaxation from care, after their day's work is done. Recreation is as necessary for work to the average person, and the management of the mills takes pleasure in providing a suitable place for it.

Mr. Firth wished to convey to the employees the message of good will from his father, the President of the Firth Carpet Company. Only Doctor's orders prevented him from again making the trip to the mills here, as that was one his dearest wishes. Whether he would be able at some future time to do so, he could not, of course, tell, but at present it was impossible.

Mr. Firth felt sure, however, that he was with him in thought and spirit that evening. As his gift to the club, Mr. T.F. Firth had directed that his son select a library of volumes of both solid and light reading to be paid for by the elder gentleman, and to be his tribute towards furnishing the new club house. Prolonged applause greeted this announcement.

Mr. Firth. Also bore the hearty good wishes of his brother who was here this past summer, and who would have been greatly pleased to be present on this occasion, though it was impossible for both of them from England at the same time.

After further felicitous expressions, Mr. Firth closed his remarks with the following words:

In is spirit of appreciation of the good will of all, from the highest to the lowest, who have contributed to the success of our enterprise, and will in the spirit of gratitude to Providence for the prosperity we have enjoyed, I now, in the name of the trustees of the Firth Carpet Company, declare this club open."

Mr. Firth next called upon Mr. F. J. Collier, who has been present at Firthcliffe on previous occasions. Mr. Collier was enthusiastically received, and responded in a speech of mingled with and patriotism. He thought as some of the people there had endured flood of waters, it would be the refinement of cruelty to subject them now to a flood of speeches. He spoke briefly, but eloquently, calling attention to the flags at the rear of the stage, emblematical of the Anglo-American unity and strength and "peace and honor" as the motto of both nations. He closed with the following little verse and paraphrase which simply brought down the house:

"Show me a Scotchman who doesn't love the thistle.
Show me an Englishman who doesn't love the Rose.
Show me a true hearted son of old Erin who doesn't
love the land where the Shamrock grows.
Show me a Weaver who doesn't love his shuttle;
Show me a working man who doesn't love his tools;
Show me the true-hearted son of endeavor who doesn't
love the spot where the Firth name rules.

Mr. Firth then called upon Mr. B.F. Tobey, as the selling of the company, one of the most important factors in their prosperity. Mr. Tobey responded very pleasantly, speaking of the necessity of the united effort on the part of both employees and selling agent, the one to make goods first class and saleable, and the other to find a market for the products. He closed by graceful words of congratulations to all concerned upon the opening of the club.

The Hon. John Orr was then called upon. He spoke of the pride Cornwall people and Orange County residents feel for the Firth Carpet mills and great benefit the industry is to the town of Cornwall. He was glad to the privilege afforded thus publicly to express the sentiment of the townspeople and to bear witness to the high regard in which both the firm and the employees.

His remarks were brought to a close with congratulatory words to the beneficiaries of the club and to its vice president.

Mr. Firth then called upon Mr. John Nolan, representing the employees. Mr. Nolan, with his characteristic versatility spoke most effectively. He gently informed the listeners that he was neither a Depew nor a Firth, not a Collier, not an Orr, and he hoped they would be lenient with him as he hadn't a great command of the English language.

Soberly, he had been asked on behalf of the employees of the Firth Carpet Company to express their appreciation of the many favors they received at their hands, and for those in store, in the way of enjoyment of the new club house. He had been employed by the firm some sixteen years, and had found them always ready and anxious to favor their employees in every way possible. The employees had had many evidences of the firm's kindness and generosity toward them, and this latest gift will be especially appreciated and enjoyed. He wished to thank the firm and the staff of Directors for their uniform courtesies toward their employees, and with a hearty with Mr. Firth, Mr. Nolan retired from the stage. Mr. Firth then suggested that the floor be cleared for dancing. This was soon done and strains of music from Butterworth's orchestra commenced, and the dance was in full swing.

In the meantime, guests were being seated at the banquet tables, spread in the lower rooms where Caterer Duncan of Newburgh had charge. A sumptuous repast was served to between four and five hundred persons. The Firthcliffe band was of course in attendance at the club house and contributed their share towards the evening's pleasure in a musical way.

Besides the officials of the mill and their wives, and the employees of when there were about four hundred, those present included Rev. Dr. Allen; Rev. Dr. Page; C.C. Cocks; H. N. Clark; G.B. Mailer; F.C. White; H.C. Woodworth; J.S. Holloran; H. J. Van Duzer; G.T. Peckham; W. H. Chadeayne; D.L. Orr; Harry Van Duzer; Edw-Hunter; John Orr; J, B. Dickerson and daughter; L. Goodnough and wife; William Chadeayne; and wife; James Broadhead; J.A. Tappan; Charles H. Mead; Thomas Taft; H.R. Taylor; Frank Mead; J.N. Noe; J.H. Ward; William Preston; G. M. Hayward; Harry Hancon; Jos. Broadhead; Dr. S.D. Harrison; Dr. D. H. Chandler; T.H. Rea; S. Emslie;

H. O. Brewster; Wm. Hollett; John Lawrence; Floyd Mailer; Charles Mailer; Rowland Cocks.

The management of the opening regretted extremely that lack of room prevented them from inviting many more of the townspeople. They would have been only too pleased to entertain a much larger number of them, had the capacity of the hall permitted. As it was, it was taxed to its utmost.

The Firthcliffe club house

The Firthcliffe Club House and Library is a present from the Firth Carpet Company to its employees. The building was erected from plans drawn by a New York architect, under the direction of Mr. James H. Aspinall, with Mr. John Preston as Foreman. The main building is 30 by 60 feet. The foundation and ground floor is of brick, and the first and second stories are wood. All floors are of the best maple flooring, and the ceilings are of Cypress. The rooms are all wainscoted. A piazza twelve feet wide extends the entire front of the building.

The lower floors have one billiard and one pool room, with first class tables for each of these games; one reading room and one card and smoking room and two shower baths. On the ground floor also are the Janitor's living rooms; Mr. Ernest Downsbrough will live there and have charge of the building. The building is supplied with town water and electric lights, and heated by steam. William Peck had charge of the plumbing.

The Library is furnished with a representative collection of the works of standard authors, as a gift from Mr. Firth, President of the Firth Carpet Company. The tables are all of quartered oak, also magazine and newspaper racks with over thirty daily, weekly and monthly publications on file. The card and smoking room is furnished with quartered oak card tables and a number of games. Upstairs is a large auditorium with a seating capacity of 380. On this floor is also a ladies dressing room.

The building containing the bowling alley is of brick and ninety feet long. The alleys themselves are first class and were constructed by the Brunswick-Balke-Collender Company.

Persons not employees of the Firth Carpet Mills can become members of the club by communicating with the secretary, Mr. H. Gugelmann, and by payment of $2.00 per year. The entire building and its furnishings are arranged with a view to convenience, entertainment and elegance, with no expense spared anywhere that could contribute father to any of these conditions. In this princely gift to their employees, the Firth Carpet Company has only followed the precedent they themselves established of doing nothing by halves. "The best is none too good" seems always to be their motto, and it is a matter of much pride and pleasure to Cornwall people to claim the firm, its officials, and employees as citizens and friends."

END

For the full story on growing up around Firthcliffe, the Firth mill and the Firthcliffe clubhouse see Ed Smith's recollections starting on page 191.

Back in the day when you bought a car there was no driver education, you learned on your own. The driver of the first car in Firthcliffe, (the owner I only know, as the story was retold to me, as Percy) went by the club waving to everyone, then he went by again, then again. Finally, someone yelled to him: "Percy, what the H- you doing?" Percy's reply was: "I don't know how to get it outta gear, I'm waiting for it to run out of gas!"

Firth, Sir Thomas Freeman [1829-1909]
Son of Edwin Firth of Hockmonwike

He went into partnership with his brother-in-law – J. W. Willans to found Firth, Willans & Company of Hockmonwike. In 1867, they bought a disused worsted mill at Bailiff Bridge. In 1875, John Willans left the partnership and the company became T. F. Firth & Company.

On 15th February 1854, he married Hannah Maria Willams. He was the First Baronet Aykroyd of Lightcliffe. In 1909, his son, Algernon, succeeded to the title.

He was a life-long member of the local Congregational community. A Liberal, he was involved in the life and welfare of Bailiff Bridge and the surrounding district.

He lived at The Flush, Hockmonwike

Firth, Sir Algernon Freeman [1856-1936]
Born on 15th September 1856, the son of T. F. Firth. He was the second baronet and, because there were no sons, the baronetcy became extinct.

He entered the family firm and was subsequently Chairman of T. F. Firth & Company until his retirement in 1921, when Sir William Aykroyd took over, ending the Firth family connection with the carpet business. He was instrumental in establishing a branch factory at Firthcliffe. In 1881, he married Janet Gertrude Lindsay. Children: Dorothy Gertrude. He and Lady Janet were benefactors for the district. The family lived at Holme House and maintained the family tradition of a close relationship with their employees. In May 1889, he contributed towards a fund for tenants who had been evicted from their homes in Ireland. In 1911, they donated George V Park, and a drinking fountain which stood at Bailiff Bridge.

He was president of the local Liberal association. He was president of the Association of British Chambers of Commerce until 1918. He was High Sheriff of Yorkshire

[1922-1923]. When he retired after World War I, he and his wife went to live at Scriven Park, Knaresborough, where he died. People were reported to be weeping in the streets when they left the district.

1911 Christmas card found in the Firth files *Cornwall Historical Society*

Dear Friend :-

There are few voices like the voice of Christmas.

Coming down through the years, that voice is like the tones of a trumpet, bidding us behold the "glory of God in the face of Jesus Christ."

There in the crude cattle-stall—most unlikely of all places to the fancy of men—heaven's gift was laid down.

In that gift we recognize the astounding wonder of the ages; the "mystery of godliness begun in the incarnated person of the ever blessed God."

What a revolutionizing fact is this! From the advent, time is reckoned anew; light has come to the nations, and through its potency the course of the world's history has been changed.

In the memory of angels how fragrant that event must be which brought them singing, to earth! And in the hearts of men what gratitude should be awakened by the comtemplation of this sublime miracle of grace!

Is there a day in all the calendar of human events that means more of blessing for the world than Christmas Day?

Surely the causes for devout Thanksgiving are many at this hallowed season.

With best wishes for a happy, holy Christmas, I am,

Faithfully yours,

James Louis Hynes.

Cornwall Press/Cornwall Local:
April 21, 1921

"The Ward and Fanning dances which have been so successful at the old Homestead pavilion since May 25, 1917, will be given hereafter in the hall of Firthcliffe club. These young dance managers claim that they have discovered the right kind of a hall with the right kind of a floor to accommodate the large dances which they intend to stage.

Ward and Fanning have been very heroic in undertaking to handle first class public dances that have now become known as the most popular affairs of the summer season. It was Ward and Fanning who first introduced to the town of Cornwall the celebrated jazz band which has put life into the feet of all the citizens ranging from ten years of age to the golden age of eighty. If it had not been for Ward and Fanning the dancing art would have died in Cornwall but instead of dying it has resurrected the youthful spirit of all the folks and reinvigorated gentlemen who would have fallen into the grave. It is no uncommon sight now to witness ladies and gentlemen seventy five and eighty years of age kicking across the smooth surface of the ballroom floor and resembling the gaiety of the mountain goat. The Ward and Fanning dances this season at Firthcliffe are bound to draw big crowds."

May 28, 1927

"Band concerts will again be held this year in Firthcliffe. The concerts are sponsored and paid for each year by the Firth Carpet Company. A new band stand will be erected shortly. It will be built on the Firth Carpet Company's property near the Firthcliffe Club House of which the carpet company is also the owner. The old band stand, which is located on the opposite side of the road, was on private property and has been removed as the owner will build a store in its place. The new stand will be built between the Firthcliffe Club House and the Jennings home.

Jesse Butter worth is the leader of the band and has given fine concerts for years. The concerts are greatly enjoyed through the summer months, drawing greater numbers each time from Firthcliffe and many in cars from the surrounding neighborhood. Mr. Butterworth, with the exception of a few short periods has been leader of the Firthcliffe band for more than twenty years."

Firth club would survive a fire in December of 1951. When Mohasco Industries bought Firth Carpet in the early 1960's (See full story on page 149) the Firthcliffe club would be given by Mohasco to the Cornwall Hospital. Mr. and Mrs. Sal Marci would buy the club from the hospital a short time after, running a modern restaurant and reopening the bowling alley which had been closed by Mohasco. This would keep the clubhouse in operation until it was gutted by a fire in October of 1970.

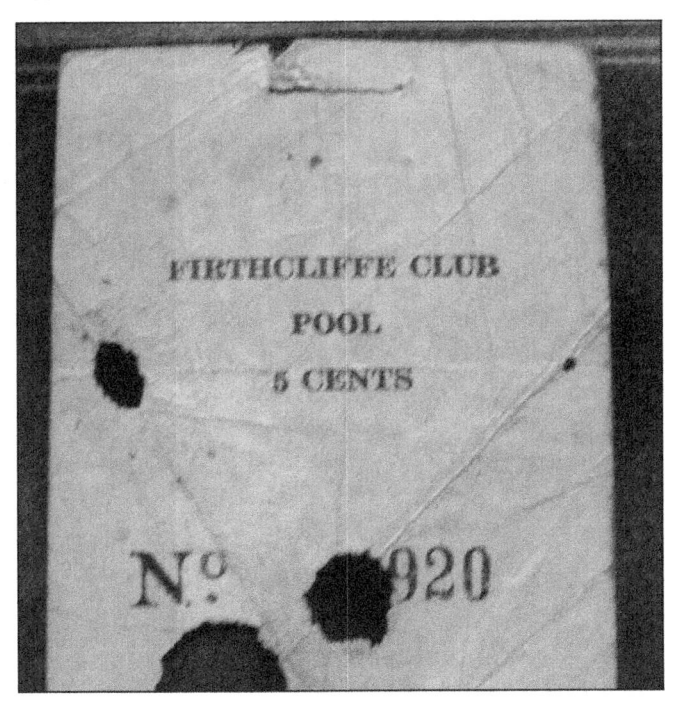

Pool ticket, Firthcliffe club
Five tickets gave you a free game of pool
Frank Dabroski

My grandfather's shaving mug from
Bob Smith's clubhouse barber shop
These were for sale for everyone, with
the last mane in gold leaf.
Bob Smith's photo is on page 253

Chapter Six:
The Aqueduct
October 20, 1910

"Men in the employee of the Board of Water supply of New York started to erect a private telephone line throughout the length of the aqueduct. The poles are now being installed along the line.

The line will be a private telephone line and will be of immense service along the aqueduct as it will enable the men on either end of the line to keep posted in regard to work on the other. The line stretches through Westchester, Putnam, Orange and Ulster Counties, from New York City to the Catskills."

From 1907 until 1917 a project was underway that, in size and scope, was equaled only by the building of the Panama Canal. The work began with New York City's Mayor McClellan turning the first spade of earth at the reservoir near Peekskill on Thursday, June 20th, he and his party having arrived on the steamboat *Albany.* Everything about the new aqueduct was to be on a colossal scale. The building of the the Ashokan Reservoir high in the Catskills would entail the building of a dam 220 feet high to contain the waters of the Esopus, Schoharie, Catskill creeks and the Rondout River, making for a reservoir 12 miles in length, The Ashokan would have a capacity of 120.000.000.00 gallons of water when filled. Linking this massive body of water with New York City would be a pipe described in the press as a gravity driven pipe 80 miles in length and big enough "to carry a railway train."

The work force, from policemen to blacksmiths to the sandhogs who would actually do the digging for this immense undertaking, could have matched in size the greatest armies of the day. The lives of the people who lived in the path of this juggernaut were changed forever as whole towns were condemned and flooded and graveyards moved.

The following appeared in the Newburgh News in June of 1910, the age and quality of the copy made it impossible to rewrite the whole story and at verbatim:

"Aqueduct Commission no.7 has filed its second separate report covering eleven parcels of land taken by the City of New York for the new Aqueduct in Cornwall.

The total amount in damages in this report amount to $17.950, and the total recommendations for expenses to $1. 250.90 is as follows:

No. 360, Claimant George C. Abell, claim $500.00, award. $250.00, expenses, $115.00, Attorney, H.W. Chadeayne............"

The condemning of land has a personal attachment to it because a member of my family grew up on one of the farms in the town of Olive Bridge that was to be flooded over. One of the stories of those times and carried down through the years in my family is both sad and chilling. The pine box of one of the graves being moved had deteriorated to the point that upon being removed it fell apart, exposing a young girl in a bright blue dress and beautiful blond hair. No sooner had this young lady been exposed to the air once again her than her body literally turned to dust.

The construction would move through Vails Gate, Firthcliffe and then through Cornwall before plunging below the Hudson River. Two shafts were dug in Vails Gate, Shaft 3 was in Firthcliffe; Shaft 4 was near Mailer Avenue (the "slate banks" as they are known-the piles of cast off slate from the shaft, can still be seen today) Shafts 5 to 8 were in Cornwall on Hudson and near the banks of the Hudson. Shaft three had a compressor plant to run the pneumatic drilling equipment and ventilation for the workers more than a thousand feet down.

Severe damage but no loss of life would occur at Shaft 6 from a dynamite accident. "Popping rock" caused from the great pressure of the ground so far down would take its toll on the work force. Several of the aqueduct workers died in horrible accidents on the railroad tracks from trying to board passing trains on the West Shore Railroad.

(Top) Exact measuring under the Hudson, 1907 (Bottom) 1911 drilling the shaft

113

Catskill Aqueduct
Moodna pressure tunnel
View at top of Shaft 7
Hudson River about 150 feet below
Contract 20
February 16, 1910

*Photo credits: The New York Public Library
Digital Collection*

Throughout the construction the papers would recount stories of progress in the tunnel and arrests made by the aqueduct police force for drunkenness and fights and even murder.

The final rock barrier was broken through in April of 1912. Then the massive job of lining the entire tunnel with concrete was begun. Six hundred million gallons of water a day could start flowing through the immense tunnel on the way to the city which in the end cost over 187 million dollars to construct.* At the time work was begun predictions were that the work would still be going on into the 1930's.

The expansion of this system would continue through the 1950's. Even at this date (2010) a new water tunnel is underway under New York City to as a replacement for an aging tunnel that has worked year round, twenty four hours a day and without incident for a nearly a hundred years.

Sources-Newburgh Daily News/Newburgh Free Library; "Cornwall, N.Y. Images from the past" 1988

Ashokan Dam, the two captions read:
"Showing Big Tonche and Overlook Mts. Catskill, N.Y.
"New York City Boulevard on top of Ashokan

Ghosts of the O&W: Remains of the O&W's Orrs Mill coal pier, 1965

Walter Kierzkowski

Chapter Seven:
Orrs Mills/
Orrs Mills North

"The O. & W. R.R. bridge over Murderers creek at Orrs Mills, in the town of Cornwall, will be one of the largest railroad trestles in this country. It will be over 1,200 feet long and 150 feet high. This is 380 feet longer than the great suspension bridge at Niagara, 25 feet higher than High Bridge over the Harlem River, higher than the Brooklyn Bridge* and larger than the new bridge over the Thames. It is supported between the abutments by two huge piers and fifteen iron columns."

Cornwall Reflector December 24, 1881

The limestone for the abutments, cut from a quarry in New Hamburg, was shipped by scow to the Mead and Taft docks at Cornwall. *Cornwall Reflector*

* Orrs Mills bridge saw its first train on January, 8th 1883
The Brooklyn Bridge opened that following may.

Orrs Mills trestle would be built new with double track between 1902 and 1904. It was single tracked in 1946, and scrapped in 1962.

"In 1845 John Orr first arrived in Cornwall and began operating the grist mill on the Moodna that up until that time had been under ownership of the Townsend family. William Orr joined his brother in the business soon after. William would replace the old Townsend home with a spacious home of his own and add taking in summer boarders as additional means of income to Orr's number of already thriving enterprises. The house was advertised as "A three minute walk to the station, five minutes to the Erie station, three miles from the West Shore Railroad; rates one to two dollars per day."*

Source: Cornwall, N.Y. Images from the past 1988

"William Orr, Esq. is painting his house inside and out, also his large flouring mill, barns, stables and making many other improvements, giving a large force of men employment, and by so doing benefitting others as well as himself."

Cornwall Reflector, 1883

In May, 1881 the three articles below appeared on the same page together in the *Cornwall Reflector:*

"Another accident on the West Shore Railroad, near old Storm King, resulted in the death of two laborers, and the injury of two others. They were run over by the construction train Wednesday morning.

"The Railroad bridge over the Moodna near Orrs Mills is nearly completed. The rapidity with which the work on the West Shore and O&W Railroads is being pushed is favorable to the announcement that cars will be running over them by the first of January."

There is also a local mention of William Orr treating his guests to a straw ride around Cornwall

(Top) Passing over the first Moodna trestle, circa 1900
(Bottom) Orrs Mills station at the far end

All three trestle photos and station drawing: Joe Bux, O&WRHS

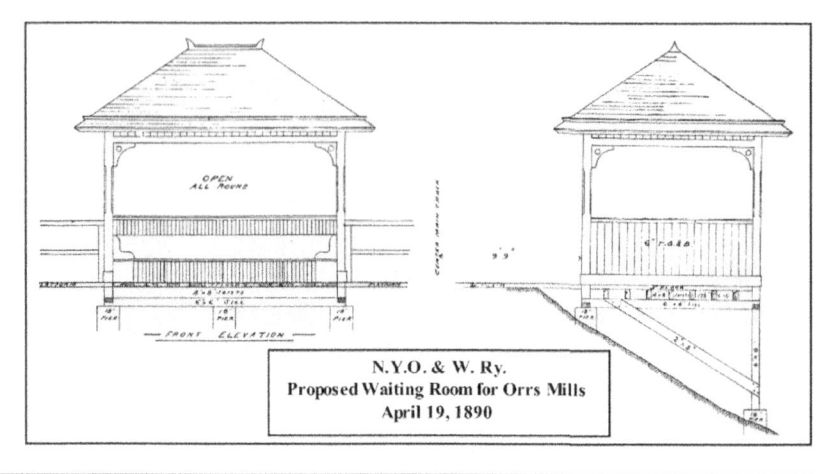

**N.Y.O. & W. Ry.
Proposed Waiting Room for Orrs Mills
April 19, 1890**

Corner of State road (Creek Road, today's Rt. 32) and Road to Cornwall (Montana Road/Quaker Ave) The road from Cornwall split into a wye to join the state road, the other point of the wye being right where the road disappears in the distance. The highway bridge over Moodna would be just out of sight in the distance, with the O&W's trestle4 beyond that.

Cornwall Local, 1903:

"The horse and road Association, of Orange County, held a monthly meeting at Mr. Harriman's office in New York. Among those in attendance were Senator and Supervisor L.F. Goodsell; Supervisors Moshier, Loughran, Fredericks and Padleford. As a result the Board of Supervisors are to meet in special session Friday, the 24th, to do its part in forwarding the good roads project in Orange County. Supervisor Orr will be present.

The association believes it can, with the co-operation of the Supervisors, get $400,000 expended in road improvements by the aid of the state and contributions from the railroads so that the only taxation will be on $60,000 county bonds. A sufficient sinking fund being secured to care for the principal as it matures."

Good Roads for Cornwall

"One of our exchanges still persists in saying that Cornwall is not "in it" on the road question. If the Editor of said paper would study his geography a little more he would find out that the "Newburgh to Woodbury line" which he so glibly quotes at the head of the list of highways to be improved this year, goes through the center of the town of Cornwall, and that the town of Cornwall gets six miles of improved roads, as noted in our last issue."

From the Cornwall Press: March 16, 1921:

"The Fox Film Company is staging a scene for one of their movies on the creek road on the property belonging to Wilfred Wood. A temporary bridge will be built bridging the creek, and a truck will be blown up while crossing it under its own power. Several other places were investigated, including a few in Moodna, but none seemed as good a location as the one secured.

Alongside the new concrete abutment was a coal bunker operated by the Orrs and serviced by the railroad. The remnants of the coal bunker would survive into the 1970's.

Ron Vassallo, O&WRHS

A view of Wm. Orrs Mill, and the original Orrs Mills trestle
(Below) Postcard of Orrs Mill and dam, the trestle is seen over the mill.

(Top) Rebuilding the Moodna bridge *O&WRHS* The concrete piers for the new trestle can be seen to the right. One of the original footings in the picture above is seen in the picture below.

The following two articles are from
The *Newburgh Daily News*

June, 1910:

"Newburghers who ride in automobiles or carriages will be glad to learn that the dangerous curve in the Road at Orr's Mills is to be eliminated. Thanks to the generosity of the venerable William Orr, the high bank which skirts the road on the south side, completely cutting off all view of drivers or pedestrians, is to be removed and the road widened at this point to ensure safety. Mr. Orr has made this improvement possible by presenting a strip of his property adjoining the road to the county. County Engineer Smith will proceed at once with the work and it is hoped that in the very near future this curve, which has so long been a menace to the safety of all persons who traverse the road, will be no more.

Mr. Orr and his sons tell of many hair-breadth escapes they have witnessed and say that the relief from the constant strain they are under will more than compensate for their property."

August 20, 1910:

"The O&W railroad is to have a night watchman to patrol its tracks between Orr's Mills and Moodna, to see that no more rails are loosened from the ties, as happened last Sunday night, when a serious accident might have occurred had the rails not been seen by some workmen in time."

*Next three pages: Orrs Mills Trestle:
With a view of the mill below, the same view today, and the same photo from my drawing*

Year 1908

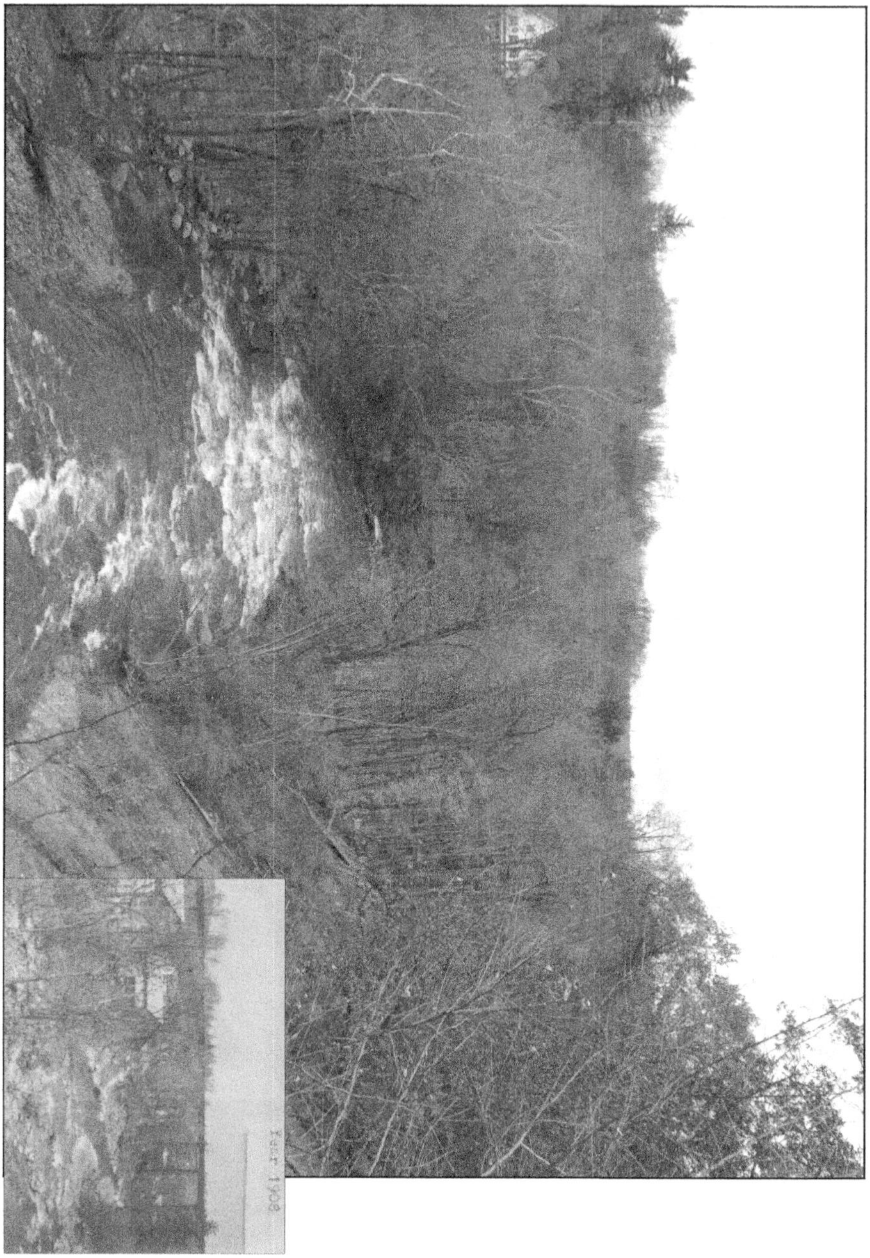

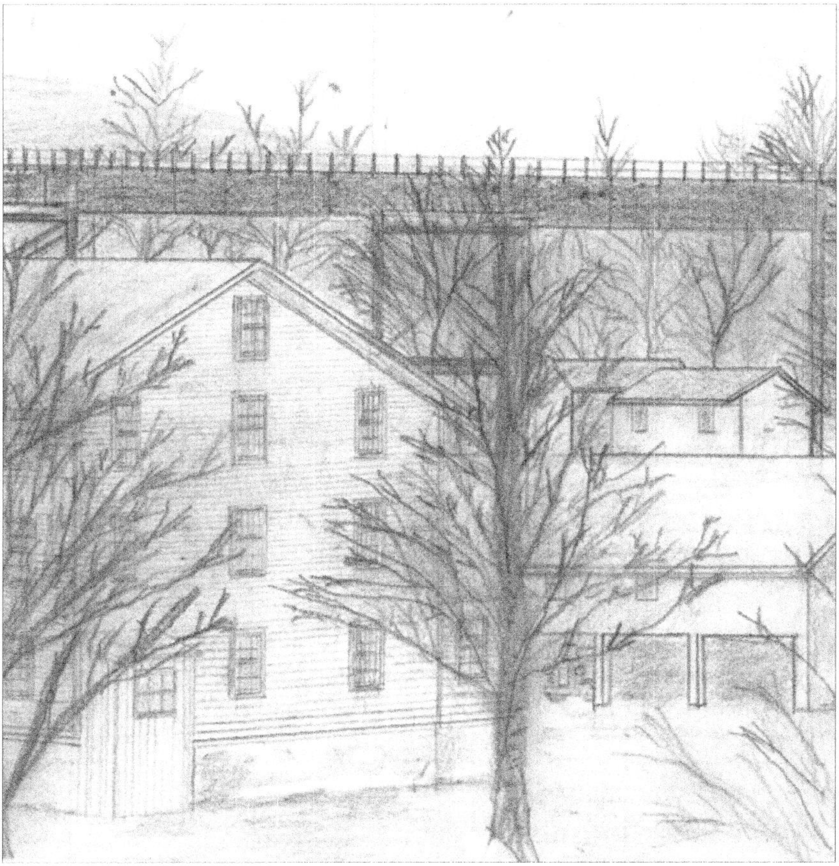

SITE OF ORR'S MILLS ESTABLISHED YEAR OF 1776. SERVED AMERICAN ARMIES FROM WASHINGTON TO PERSHING

Marker by Rt. 32, Dedicated on Aug. 16, 1956, a gift to Walter Orr by "three of his close friends" as described in the Cornwall Local. The three friends and Mr. Orr were at the dedication ceremony and were as follows: Col. Gustave Matzman, retired president of the New York Central Railroad; Harold H. Burns, proprietor of Wadley & Smythe Florists, located at 55th Street and Park Avenue, New York City; B.K. Wild, sales manager of the General Motors Corporation, Overseas division.

Walter S. Orr blamed the closing of the famous Orrs Mill on the Model "T" and the coming of the motion picture. Before they came on the scene, Mr. Orr explained, the men would go out of the house after dinner to play with their "fancy chickens". The raising and exhibiting of these chickens in shows was a hobby which helped kept the mill in business. Once the Model T and the movies arrived, wives and children were asking Father to take them out on drives and to the movies, leaving little time for taking care of chickens

For the dedication of the Orrs Mills marker in 1956 the Cornwall Local remembered: "The small home where Tom

Brophy lived at the rear of the mill was demolished. Tom drove the Orr's feed wagon and was a very special person to all the small boys in town who used to hook rides with him as he made his rounds to the livery stables and chicken coops", according to the recollection of Wm. B. Cocks.

September 27, 1917:
THINK A MOMENT
"We know that is very tough sledding now in the poultry raising. We do not advise ant to raise more than they can afford to feed well. Grains are high and corn will stay up no doubt. Don't keep a bird that is not worthwhile. The crop of young chicks this year is at least 50% short and the old stock is at least 50% short, so it would seem to us that those who have them will be paid well. But don't keep and loafers in the yard. Be careful, don't waste: things will be all right."
WM. ORR & SONS
Phone 144 Orr's Mills, N.Y.

This article would fall right in with Walter Orr's explanation on
of the decline of Orr's Mill, followed by the leasing of the mill to "Fibre Cooperage Corporation" a few years later (Page 123) The realignment of Rt. 32 in the 1930's would be the final chapter in the Orr's Mill story. A major change in the local business landscape and local color was underway as the 1920's drew near.

In the April, 3, 1931 edition of the Cornwall Local would note: "Work has been started on the new Vails Gate-Woodbury Road. The old mill at Orrs Mills has been torn down and the buildings are being moved to make way for the new bridge which will be constructed across the creek.

From the Cornwall Press, August 10, 1921:
Fibre Cooperage Corporation
Orrs Mills, N.Y.
INCORPORATED UNDER THE LAWS OF
THE STATE OF NEW YORK

For several years past there has been a great demand for a substitute for wooden butter tubs, pails and barrels. This company controls the patent rights to manufacture these products from fibre, successfully used in Germany for many years, being less in cost in weight and higher in efficiency.

For this purpose the property at Orr's Mills, including mill, warehouses and water power have been leased for a term of years with an option of buying. Machinery is now being installed and preparations are made to start manufacturing.

An exceptional opportunity presents itself to local investors to participate in this home industry.

The unsold portion of the Preferred Eight Per Cent and Common Stock of this corporation is offered for a limited time at $50.00 per share each.

Information may be obtained and subscriptions made through M. Hennings or J.C. McMurray at the factory or at the real estate office of W.H. Stone, Cornwall, N.Y.

Call or phone- Cornwall 114-J1-4
Factory telephone- 116-J1-4

Cornwall Public Library

Once the railroad closed in '57, Orrs Mills' largest landmark became just one more massive job for the scrap crew. The following is from the Cornwall Local on Feb 3, 1962:

"I.E. Wilcox of Roscoe, N.Y.; was one of three contractors who purchased the O&W's 169 bridges for scrapping. The steel went to a Belgium firm and was shipped overseas 4,000 tons at a time, the firm outbidding all U.S. scrap metal buyers. The scrapping of the Moodna trestle will take about three months."

Cornwall Local, Cornwall Public Library

March 15th, 1962: Orrs Mills trestle comes down

Except for the massive trestle abutment alongside present day Rt. 32, which is visible only in the fall and winter, little remains visible from a passing car to tell a railroad bridge ever existed here. With both the mill and the trestle vanished from the landscape, the following lament of the Cornwall Local in 1956 over the loss of the mill still rings true fifty years later:

"The cars speed along faster than ever on Rt. 32 and though occasionally an alert motorists may catch a glimpse of the new marker, the glories of Orrs Mills, with its buildings "picturesquely situated near the road leading from Cornwall station and Canterbury are forever lost in the speed of this era."

Next page: Rebuilding the Orrs Mills Trestle, circa 1904 *O&WRHS*

The construction of the new bridge was built around the old steelwork, which can still be seen to the right, using the old bridge as a construction platform.

The lower photo is the same site today.

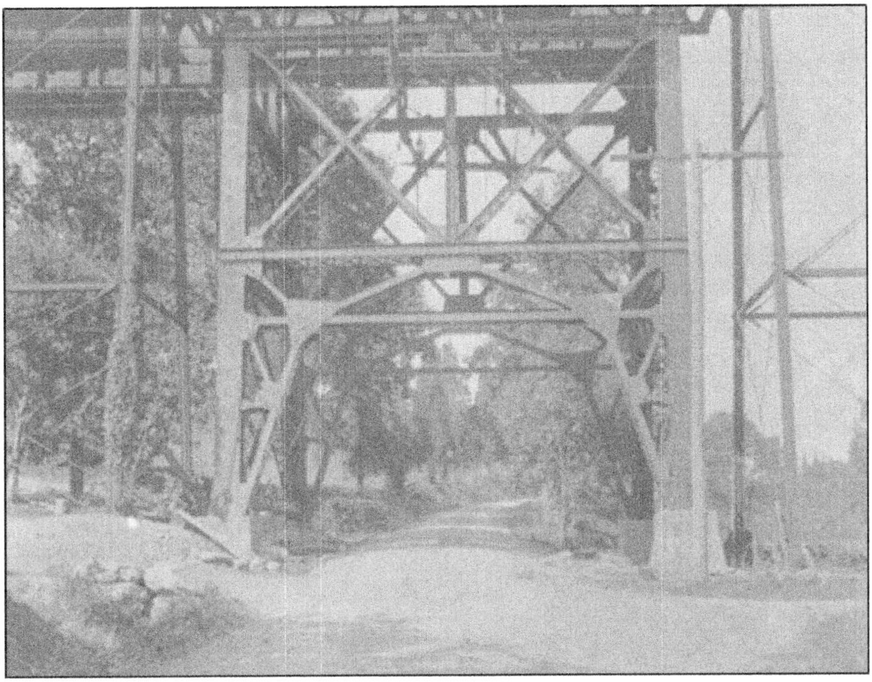

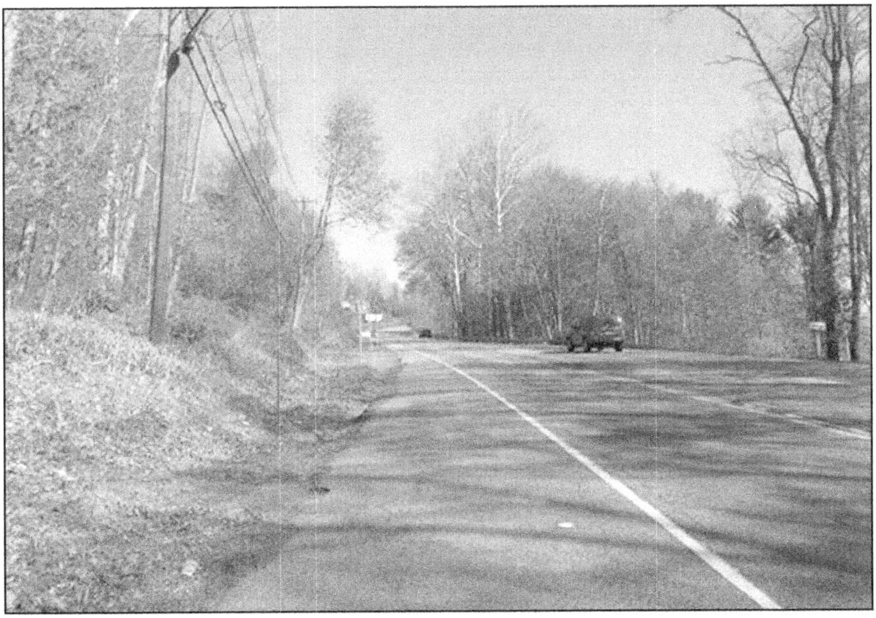

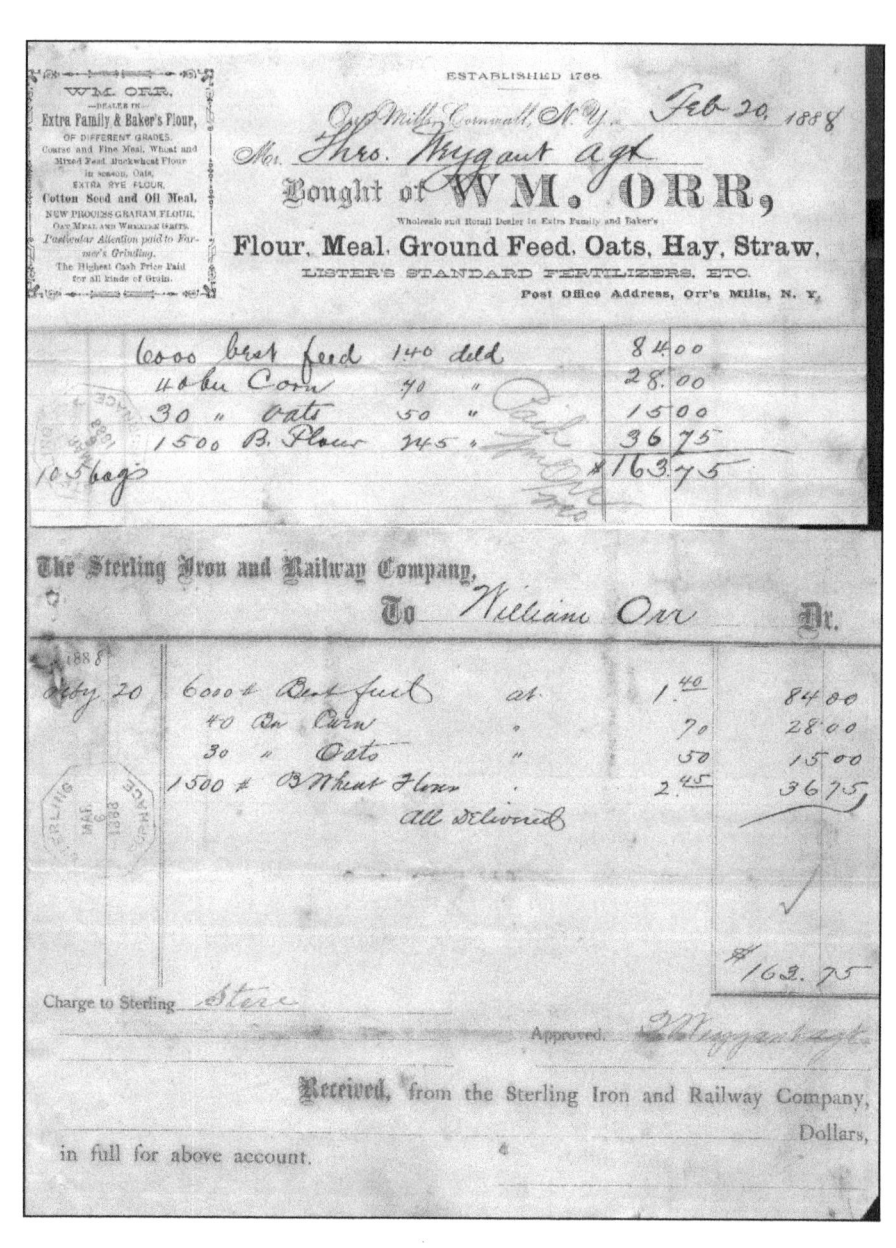

Receipt from Orr's Mill, 1888, to the Sterling Iron and Ry. Company *Author's collection*

WM. ORR & SONS,

Wholesale and Retail Dealers in Extra Family and Bakers' Flour,

Meal, Ground Feed, Oats, Hay and Straw. Jermyn Lackawanna and Old Companies Lehigh Coal, Fertilizers, etc.

P. O., ORR'S MILLS, N. Y.

Established 1766, under present control 50 years.

Muller's 1903 Orange County Atlas

The old dam at Orrs Mills
Spring, 2019

Above Orrs Mills the O&W made a 90 degree turn before crossing over the Erie's two Newburgh branches: Over the "shortcut" and under the Newburgh branch proper.[4]

The New York State Thruway would be constructed between the branches in the 1950's. Bottom: The site of the O&W bridge over the shortcut

Ray Kelly

---

[4]My two books "Schunemunk and Shortcuts", and "Ski trains, Trackcars and Trails" cover the history of the Erie Railroad's Newburgh branches in better detail than can be mentioned here.

139

Above: A northbound O&W freight climbs the uphill curve between Orrs Mills and Meadowbrook. The bridge over the shortcut lies directly ahead.
Walter Kierzkowski
Below: On the Newburgh branch- Erie 447 has the Newburgh "Haul" crossing the bridge over the O&W, circa 1960's
Dennis Carpenter

Meadowbrook station, prior to construction of the highway overpass

O&WRHS/Jeff Otto

Passing southbound (by timetable) under the overpass, bell ringing as she approaches Meadowbrook station

Jeff Otto/O&WRHS

(Top) Adv. #3 passing through Little Britain on 8/30/41, (Bottom) Engine 406, one of the O&W's "Mountain" type locomotives, 4-8-2 wheel arrangement, at Middletown station, waiting to take its run north

The Cornwall Way freight at Livingston
Manor behind #225

Engine number 39, once the pride of the line
She still rounds the bend in this aging mind
Feels like thunder lifting the ground
Smoke, steam and bark, oh how I can still hear the sound
39 is a ghost, she's here, she's downtrack gone
Sidebars fly, steel wheel and track joints pound!

At night, Oh! What a show!
Headlight in the night, orange cab a-glow

Engineer waving from the cab, master of all
Throaty whistle blows, she's a mile gone!

I hear her at sunrise, I hear her at night
I hear her amid storms and know all is alright

Oh where did that engine of my childhood go?
Around the curve to where in my memories, I hear a whistle blow

I will know I have reached heaven's door
When I hear that throaty whistle in the night once more

"...Wedding bells will ring so merrily
Every tear will be a memory
So wait and pray, each night for me
'till we meet again"

"Till we meet again"- 1918
Richard A. Whiting

Chapter Eight:
World War One

Like the rest of America, Firthcliffe Carpet Company and its employees would weather good times and bad: War and peacetime, boom times, lean years and otherwise. Starting below is a timeline of events in the lifetime of Firthcliffe and the Firth Carpet Company as the headlines read in the pages of the Cornwall Reflector/Cornwall Local.

November, 17, 1884: Montana Woolen Mills reopen as Firth Carpet.

April: Looms coming from England

November 20, 1886: Firth Carpet Mills now in operation. Firth to build some thirty houses. Superintendent Fred Booth arrives from England to head the mill.

1887: Brick engine house completed.

June, 1891: Mammoth chimney erected.

March, 1893: Frozen mill race closes mill until April.

June, 1898: Auction in New York City floods market with cheap carpeting, forcing Firth Carpet to close "for a few weeks".

March, 30, 1899: 50' x 150' building being erected, 200,000 bricks are ordered from Hedges Brickyard in Cornwall.

December, 1, 1904: New water wheels christened "Dorothy" and "Mary".

December 16, 1905: Engine plant being electrified.

March 18, 1909: Algernon Firth draws resolution congratulating Taft on being elected President.

March 14, 1912: Firth Carpet working around the clock to fill rush order for 10,000 rugs. April: Some workers on 4 day week due to slack work.

March 21, 1912; Firth to build new O&W sidetrack.

Cornwall Local, March 4, 1915:

NEW MANAGEMENT AT FIRTH CARPET MILLS

After nearly thirty years of service, Mr. Booth has tendered his resignation. Morris M. Davidson is now General Manager.

Just twenty nine years ago the present month-in March 1886, Messrs. Firth of England, bought at public auction the former Broadhead Woolen Mill property, at what as then known as west Cornwall, or Montana, now Firthcliffe. To the newly purchased mills came Mr. Fred Booth from Philadelphia as superintendent. After nearly thirty years active service in the interests of the mill, Mr. booth now retires, as briefly noted in our last issue, from the more strenuous efforts of detail management, retaining however, the position of director and secretary of the Firth Carpet Company.

Mr. Booth came to America from England in 1884, when at twenty four years of age, to open and take charge of new mills in this country, at Philadelphia, for the Firth carpet Company; and in December, 1886, came to Cornwall as a permanent resident. He was superintendent of the mills until five years ago, when he became General Manager for the Firth carpet Company, including the Firthcliffe and Auburn mills. He continued in this capacity until the close of 1914, having handed in his resignation last May.

June 21, 1917:
"A fair crowd was present at the Red Cross dance at the Firthcliffe Club last Saturday and thoroughly enjoyed the dancing to the music of Prof. Travis's Orchestra of Newburgh."

June 21, 1917:
"The Firthcliffe Homing Pigeon Society's 1,000 mile race from Greenville, Alabama, to Firthcliffe, was won by Wm. Campbell's bird. The time is unknown at present owing to the fact that the time of release in Alabama is definitely not known here."

In 1910 the U.S. Army adopted the M-1910 Haversack as the standard back pack for all infantrymen. The pack is essentially a sheet of rugged khaki-colored canvas that folds around its contents (bedroll, clothing, daily rations, and assorted personal items), and is held together by flaps and adjustable buckle-straps. The two shoulder straps are designed to attach to a web belt or suspender configuration. The exterior of the pack has loops, rings, and grommet tabs for attaching a bayonet sheath, a "meat can" (mess kit) pouch, and a canvas carrier for a short-handled shovel (aka. entrenchment tool).

This pack remained in service, most notably during World War I, until 1928 when it was superseded by the modified M-1928 pack. However, thousands of surplus M10s were issued during World War II to compensate for shortages in war-time textile production. *Wikipedia*
U.S. Army Haversack

News from May 17, 1917; "Corporal William Sachs of the machine Gun Company of the 71st regiment, New York City, was fatally injured on Monday morning in a fall from the O&W Railroad Bridge at Orrs Mills. He fell a distance of about fifty feet. He was found unconscious below the tracks by two of the guardsmen and conveyed to the camp. Later, he was taken to St Luke's Hospital, Newburgh, where he died yesterday

September 13, 1917: Firth Carpet gets Government contract for 120,000 yards of Haversack cloth*
November 15, 1917: 20 stars in Firthcliffe service flag.
December 31, 1914: Firth Carpet still going full time despite slack market during war

"Letters from Firthcliffe lad overseas" July 17, 1918:

From John Barley, Company L of the 107th Regiment to his mother, Mrs. Thomas McDermott:
July 1st
"I am a machine gunner now and believe me, it is sure some gun. Jerry is going to stop when it opens up on him.

We are all ready for the Boche any time and they are getting it all along the line. I am feeling better than I have ever felt before. They are feeding us rather well, of course, we do not expect as much as we got on the other side, but you can bet we are getting more than the Germans, and the people are good to us. They give us anything they have and do anything they can for us.
Tell dad he can tell the boys that I have been up to the front line trenches and that I like it. Mother, one of the boys from the states got lost and the Germans got him and he told him he was lost. So one of the German officers took out his compass and they took the boy back and there were three other officers and 78 Germans who came back with him. They all wanted something to eat."

July 17, 1918:
"I do not think this war will last much longer, hope not anyway. "Jerry" is not much of a shot and all we have to do is take care of ourselves and we are sure to come back safe. They gave us a gas mask and a steel hat, a "Tin Lizzie", as the boys call them. I have a machine gun which is a Lewis. I have a big Colt, also and if Jerry can get me with all that, why let him, but before he does you can bet your sweet life, mother, that he is going to remember being in a fight.

The cannons make a lot of noise but that is about all. I think after Jerry makes a few more drives he will stop, for they sure are getting killed. It seems a wonder where they all come from for after a battle the ground is covered with them. Tell all the folks around there that I send my best regards. I will do my best for my country, home, mother and my baby and friends and every one of us over here thinks the same. And you can bet that everyone from the U.S.A. will do the same."

Newburgh shipyards, 1919 the Peekskill is still on the ways, while the Cold Spring, Firthcliffe are prepared for their maiden trip.

New Windsor Town Historian

"Everyone is welcome in the yard of the Newburgh Shipyards when christening of the Firthcliffe will be launched at 11 o'clock. The sixth vessel to be launched rests on the building berth from which the SS New Windsor was released last year. Miss Margaret M. Bennett daughter of Vice President and General Manager Edwin C Bennett, will be the sponsor of Firthcliffe for which the 9000 ton named will be largely represented. The gates will be thrown open to the public at 10:45 o'clock. Following the christening a luncheon will be served, the invited guests in the formal barracks."
Newburgh Daily News May 24, 1919

The wars of the 20th century called forth boat and ship-building efforts in the Hudson Valley to serve the needs of the country in time of peril. At Kingston, Newburgh, and other river towns, vessels of various types and sizes were built. During World War I the United States Shipping Board was organized to procure vessels to meet the needs of the war effort in this country and, after a certain point, our Allies fighting in Europe and elsewhere. Wooden minesweepers and sub-chasers were built at Hiltebrant's on the Rondout. At Island Dock the Kingston Shipbuilding Company was set up to build four wooden freighters to carry cargo to our Allies abroad. At Newburgh the Newburgh Shipyards were set up to build a more ambitious group of ten steel freighters.

The World War I shipyards began their cargo ship-building efforts in mid-1917 as the United States entered the war. At Newburgh noted engineer Thomas C. Desmond acquired property just south of the city after lining up financial backing from Irving T. Bush, president of Bush Terminal in Brooklyn, and other shipping businessmen. Construction of the shipyard began in the summer of 1917 with the expansion of the property by filling in the river front. Actual building of the buildings did not begin until September 1917. Four ship building berths were constructed to build 9000 ton steel cargo ships. The first keel was not laid until March of 1918 due to a severe winter. The first ship, the *Newburgh*, was launched on Labor Day of 1918 with thousands of people in attendance and former President Theodore Roosevelt on hand to deliver a typical rousing speech. The ship was finished at the Newburgh yard and was delivered to the U.S. Shipping Board at the end of December 1918 (after the war was officially over). Shipbuilding continued with ten ships completed in total. The needs of war-torn Europe for food and other supplies, did not end with the official end of the war, so the ships being built at Newburgh and other similar yards were still needed.

The World War I cargo ships built at Newburgh were named for local towns: *Newburgh*, *New Windsor*, *Poughkeepsie*, *Walden*, *Cold Spring*, *Firthcliffe*, *Irvington*, *Peekskill*, and the last two, *Half Moon* and *Storm King* with locally inspired but not town names.

At its height the Newburgh shipyards employed 4000 workers, probably a record number for the area at any time. The majority of these workers were not originally ship builders and were trained by Newburgh Shipyards. Given that the shipyard was built from the ground up (including some of the ground,) and that the majority of workers had to be trained, the output of ten 9000 ton, 415 foot length cargo ships in two and a half years is remarkable. Among the U.S. Shipping Board Emergency Fleet Corporation shipyards established for World War I the Newburgh Shipyards was one of the more successful.

Newburgh Shipyard was a source of great local pride as well as prosperity during its years of operation from September 1917 to 1921.

Hudson River Maritime Museum

Cornwall Press, Thursday, October 14, 1918:
"Event anticipated following premature announcement of a week
ago-Whistles and bells tell glad tidings-O&W men in Parade in
forenoon-Towns big parade Monday evening-Frolic continues well into the night."

The occasion was great enough for two celebrations and we had them last Thursday, when the good news came of Germany's surrender to the allies, the people of Cornwall did justice to the great event in so far as sudden notice made possible. Bells and whistles and at evening a rattling good parade manifested the joy of the town. Some evening papers, however, carried information that the announcement was premature, to say
the least; and by next morning, everyone became aware that we celebrated too soon.
Friday, Saturday and Sunday were filled with anticipation, however, of capitulation of Germany which it was expected by most people would take place Monday morning at the latest, and pretty nearly everyone had thought out some private celebration of his or her own, to help in the general joyousness, when the good word should finally be passed along.
The coal dock whistle was the first, we believe, to announce the
wonderful news. Mead and Taft's company whistles and fire siren took up the glad refrain. The bells of the village were a little slow in getting started, but pretty soon Village Clerk F.B. King appeared with the key and got the Presbyterian Church bell busy. About this time, the liberty bell at the fire house came in on the chorus (and what here we might add that what these two bells lacked in speed at the start, they made up in continuity of performance as the gala day wore on. We doubt there if there

was a boy or girl in the village who didn't take a turn at one or the other or both of these bells some time during the day.)

By ten O'clock, employees of the O&W coal docks had arranged for a perfectly good parade and close to half a hundred strong marched two by two up River Avenue, down Hudson Street to the top of Dock Hill and return. An effort had been made to get a band, but this they were unable to secure on the short notice. They were however, led in good style by Sargent Walter Williams, Marshall Albert Hulse and Capt. Charles F.Maroney with flags flying.

A placard announcing the organization's identity was carried, in the front of the parade, while the lettering on the other signs testified to the laudable ambition of the marchers to "scrap" the Kaiser. Each man was holding onto a long rope which passed the entire length of the procession and at the rear was attached to a dummy Kaiser, who was being ignominiously drawn through the streets.

The O&W paraders included varied nationalities, colors and ages but all apparently entered into the spirit of the day with whole hearted enthusiasm and did their bit in helping along the jubilation.

Preparations were made, however, for a parade in Cornwall Monday evening and the town did itself proud in the results achieved. Mr. Fred Booth acted as Chairman of arrangements. He was assisted by town, village and various other deputies. Capt. M. Davidson of the Home Defense Corp. and Mr. John S. Halloran were Marshalls of the parade which was led by the New York Military Academy band, with the battalion of cadets, under direction of their commandant, Captain Steinbrenner who was accompanied by his staff. "

Chapter Nine:
Between the wars

Cornwall Press, December 28, 1919:

Triumphant Inauguration of Sir Algernon's Ideal British Settlement in Cornwall Fashioned Upon the English Plan of Colonization-The House a Model in Appointments for Service, Full of Meaning and Suggestion for the People of Cornwall-"God Save the King"

The ceremonies of dedication opened with 'The Star Spangled Banner" and closed with "God Save the King!" Nothing could be more democratic and condescending than that.

And the royal message from Sir Algernon read like a speech from the Throne: "Please express our pleasure at the completion and dedication of the extension of the club house for the people of Firthcliffe. We hope it will be a useful addition to the means of entertainment and enjoyment of the community's employees and form a pleasant social center for all the inhabitants of Firthcliffe."

Can there be anything more beautiful in benevolence than that.

And in the publicity matter prepared by the mill one section reads: "Every member of the working force is a member of the club. There are no dues or assessments, all expenses being met by the corporation and the BUILDING MAY BE TRULY STYLED AN ENGLISH COMMUNITY HOME."

The press went on to ask: "Not an American home? Was it for this kind of clan life that the forty-nine boys of Firthcliffe ventured their precious lives in France under the American flag?.......Is this the sort of Americanism the Firthcliffe Mill and Sir Algernon Firth would engrave upon the minds of the young men of Cornwall? Shall the people of Firthcliffe get their genuine inspiration from the carpet mill in exchange for permission to earn a living there?........."

Retuning to the letter:
"According to the official report of the mill the great ray of light at the dedication came from Colonel Bennett H. Tobey "treasurer and general salesman of the American branch." The Colonel said:
There is still to be placed in the newly completed building, which I entrust to your keeping, a bronze tablet, commemorating the service of the forty-nine boys who left the employ of the Firth Carpet Company to take their place in an Army that has brought glory to the nation and the American people."
"Colonel Tobey spoke eloquently of the great service the United States had done in coming to the rescue of the Allied forces WHEN THEY
WERE DISMAYED AND DISCOURAGED."
"Long before the hour was set for the formal opening of the new
Firthcliffe Club House the building was crowded with people employed in the mill and their families. The men were down in the bowling alleys and the roar of the bowling balls and crashing pins could be heard out in the village. Three pool tables were in action and many were waiting for their chance to enter the games.
In the large hall above the women were grouped along the walls, chatting and waiting for the ceremonies to start.
By 8'O'Clock the house was jammed and hundreds remained standing. The things of practical interest to those for whom the house was built engaged the attention of and inspection of the members of the club. That part of the building devoted to sports is thoroughly equipped with all the essential appointments and modern conveniences."
The letter goes on to describe the bowling alley as:

"The best in Orange County-the arrangements of the lights and alleys are perfect...softened and diverted so there is no glare on the eyes."

"The wide walk and lounging space will accommodate a large number of people who may wish to watch the games in the future." "Shower baths in an apartment adjoining will allow the boys to freshen up and rub down after a strenuous evening."

"Straight through the entrance opening with large wide doors stands the ball room and theatre, brilliantly illuminated, handsomely but quietly decorated."

"The highly polished hardwood dance floor has been tested on a

number of recent occasions. It is a big thing for a place like Firthcliffe.

The stage is constructed for every possible demand in service for

theatricals, concerts, or public meetings and the withdrawing and dressing rooms are large and comfortable. It would appear that the main hall will accommodate a thousand people and on Saturday night the managers of the club report more than seven hundred were present, not all seated, because space in the center had been reserved for dancing."

The letter credits the success of the new clubhouse to the intense

interest of Firth Carpet's general manager, M.M. Davidson, further going on in length with a prediction that Cornwall will one day have a central high school, universal sewer district and one universal water supply. Every "decrepit landmark" would be torn down.

Cornwall Press, January, 1920:

"The ice house of Firth's has been filled."

"The auto bus line service between Cornwall and Newburgh is equal to anything in the state. The business makes a big hole in the pocket of the West Shore

Railroad. Merchants in Newburgh hardly realize how much money this convenience carries to the town built like a toboggan slide.

Straight to Schoonmaker's store every bus goes and leaving at Grand Street and Broadway lends to that section a look of thrift."

November 4, 1920: New carpet run called "Cornwall Velvet"

November 1, 1928: New spinning mill completed.

Firth Carpet workers unloading bales of wool, date unknown

Those of us who have grown up knowing the convenience of getting
milk from just about any roadside deli or gas station are far apart from the days when milk was something of a luxury, as the following news headlines from the Cornwall Local testify:
July 26, 1900:
"Heat wave causes scarcity of milk, local boarding houses use 600 quarts daily."
"New milk law to take effect on January 1, 1915. Many dairies fear
new regulations will put them out of business."
November 1, 1928: 40 Cornwall students sick, milk source suspected
October 6, 1927: Milk dealers raise price by 2 cents to 8 cents per quart..

Firthcliffe Man Patents Clothes Dryer
Sept. 22, 1925
(Washington Bureau of News)
Washington D.C.; Sept 15-The clothes drying problem of apartment dwellers has been solved at last. Joseph Van Duzer of Firthcliffe, N.Y., has invented clothes hanging apparatus which will enable the wife to hang the clothes to the air without carrying them to the roof even though they live in an apartment. Mr. Van Duzer's invention, for which the United States Patent Office has just issued a patent, consists of a casing in the wall with a hinged supporting arm equipped with a pulley and adapted to be held in a horizontal position, providing a terminal for an endless wash line..

Storm King Highway, on the mountain between West Point and Cornwall on Hudson; opened in 1922. An engineering marvel of it's time that had been debated on and in the planning and building stages for nearly twenty years. The West Shore railroad tracks, to the right, wind their way between the base of the mountain and the Hudson River. In 1927, a 24 hour survey would count 17,000 cars on the highway between West Point and Cornwall. If each of those drivers had been buying a one dollar railroad ticket…..the impact on the railroad business was obvious.

Cornwall Local/Cornwall Public Library

CHEAP COAL
Ike: "Does your father have to pay much for coal?"
Mike: "Not a cent! We live near the railroad tracks and He makes faces at the engineers."

Firthcliffe ball field
and ball team, 1920's
Cornwall public library

FIRTHCLIFFE'S BUSY STORE

2 Cans Peas 25c

3 Jello (all flavors) 25c

2 Puffed Rice 25c

1 Sweet Clover Condensed Milk 15c

Cooked Meats

Vegetables   Fresh Fruits

Ice Cream, Soda Water, Etc.

WILLIAM C. WHYTE
GROCERIES AND GENERAL MERCHANDISE

Phone 271

FIRTHCLIFFE, N. Y.

Above and left: "Firthcliffe's Busy Store"

"Gib" McMorran's store

New Band Stand Being Built In Firthcliffe

Local Musicians Will Give Concerts in New Location This Summer—Jesse Butterworth Firth Band Leader

Band concerts will again be held this year in Firthcliffe. The concerts are sponsored and paid for each year by the Firth Carpet Company. A new band stand will be erected shortly. It will be built on the Firth Carpet Company's property near the Firthcliffe Club House of which the carpet company is also the owner. The old band stand which was located on the opposite side of the road was on private property and has been removed as the owner will build a store in its place. The new stand will be built between the Firthcliffe Club House and the Jennings home.

Jesse Butterworth is leader of the band and has given fine concerts for years. The concerts are greatly enjoyed through the summer months, drawing great numbers each time from Firthcliffe and many in cars from the surrounding neighborhood. Mr. Butterworth, with the exception of a few short periods, has been leader of the Firthcliffe Band for more than twenty-five years.

Right: Firthcliffe's bandstand

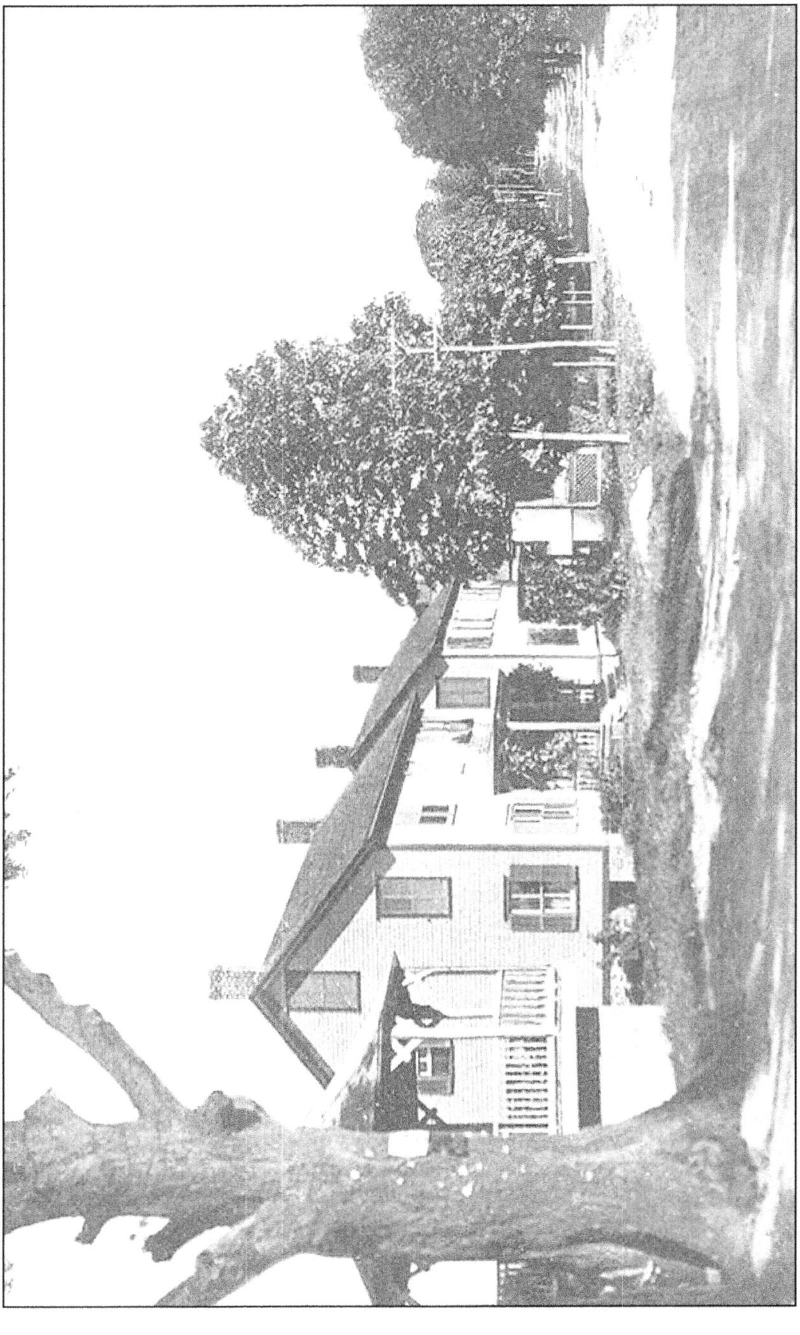

"The Firth Carpet Company Brass Band, having furnished concerts during the summer for both Firthcliffe and Cornwall, now ask those who have of listening to these concerts to help make them in making their Fourth Annual Fair a success, so that during the winter months they may be able to purchase music and instruments for another season's work.

The fair will be held in the Red Men's Hall on the evenings of September 26th, 27th, and 28th, when there will be the usual variety of useful and fancy articles sold, together with ice cream, soft drinks and cakes. There will be many contests for numerous articles, including a doll, and a large rug, 9ft by 12 ft. Music will be furnished by the band and there will be a dance each evening.

The following ladies and gentlemen have volunteered to assist:
Patronesses-Mrs. Charles H. Mead, Miss Kate Smith, Mrs. F. Booth, and Mrs. Charles Hibe.
Fancy Table-Mrs. F. Leech, Mrs. Jno Orr, Mrs. J.T. Rhoades, Mrs. Hy Van Duzer and Mrs. John Dewhirst
Cake Table_ Misses Mamie Martin, Ella Langley, and Annie McCue
Ice Cream: Mrs. John Schofield, Misses Jennie Clegg, Mary Taylor, Edna Woolsey, and Minnie Smith, Alice Clegg
Candy Table-Misses Kitty Martin, Clara Davis, Alfretta Davis, and Julia Martin
Peanuts-Misses Edna Butterworth and Maud Dewhirst
Juvenile Table-Misses Rebe Leach, Lily Halstead, and M. Herbert
Coffee Table-Mrs. Samuel Crabtree, Misses E. Clegg, and G. Crabtree
Soft Drinks-Messrs. H. Dewhirst, W. Midgley, and Arthur Sutcliffe
Door Committee-Mr. Geo. Atha, S. W. Briggs, and Hy Sutcliffe
Decorations-Mrs. J.T. Rhoades
Treasurer –Mrs. J. M. Richards
Printing-Mr. T.M. Howard
A door prize of a $5:00 gold piece"
1926

May 17, 1928 Cornwall Local/Cornwall Public library

Firth wool truck, 1920's *Doug Spaulding Collection*

(Next three pages) The Firthcliffe bowling team

One of the many family stories I heard growing up was of this one night with the bowling team. There were no electric bowling machines back in the day, pin setting or otherwise. The foul line was guarded by a referee with a whistle. The team my grandfather was on apparently never, fouled. This to the point that the referee warning's that he was going to catch one of them fouling someday was something of a running joke. Well, on this one night when the team was far enough ahead that it didn't matter my grandfather gave his teammates a "watch this" sign and purposely fouled. However, in the referee's excitement, instead of blowing his whistle, he blew into his pipe and sent ashes flying everywhere! To the laughter of the entire house!

Handsome Bowling Trophy Awarded

M. McCue Wins Silver Set for High Score at Firthcliffe Club—James Halstead is Close Second

Martin McCue won the silver set offered to the Firthcliffe Club bowlers on Saturday night. James Halstead, who won the second prize—two chickens—was a close second. He was beaten by two pins when McCue obtained three strikes in the last frame. The ten men with the highest single games of the week were in the roll-off. George Lewis and C. Hildebrandt were also close to first position.

The scores:

			Total
M. McCue	191	190	211—592
Jas. Halstead	167	242	181—590
Geo. Lewis	210	183	189—582
Hildebrandt	214	199	158—571
H. Lewis	195	192	162 549
Weeks	154	167	203—524
Richardson	182	171	169—522
A. MacDonald	162	199	158—519
H. O'Dell	146	181	165—492
E. Redfern	159	157	144—460

December 29, 1927
Cornwall Local/Cornwall Public Library

Firthcliffe bowling team
J. Richardson is in the front row, right. Martin McCue, is back row, center, Gibb McMorran front, center

A comeback from "Gib" Mac Morran to an impatient cab passenger would make the local in 1920: "Can't you go a little faster?" asked the passenger.
Unruffled, Gib replied "I could, but I have to stay with the car"

November 1, 1928: Firth Carpet's new spinning mill completed
1929: September-the Stock Market reaches a high that it will not see again for a quarter century, and then the big fall begins.
Newsboys were yelling: "Extra! Panic on Wall Street. Stock exchange closed".
"No banks are failing, that there is plenty of money about. The country and the evening meal are safe." The Bank of J.P. Morgan
By the end of the day $3,000,000,000 in market values had been wiped out.
October, 1929......................

1933: Firth shuts down power plant and connects with Central Hudson.
January 20, 1938: 900 people at Firth Carpet are laid off.
Happy days were not here again

Strikes: A group of weavers would strike in August of 1887 and October of 1891 18 female setters would strike over a reduction in wages. In October of 1907, 4 strikers were asked to move out of their housing. The credit for brining an end to this strike was given to the reasoning skills of Father Brosman of St. Thomas of Canterbury Church in Cornwall. In April of 1937 a number of Firth employees met to form "Our own union." This strike set the stage for the following story sent to me by John Tiffany:

"In 1938, to become plant engineer, after going over all of the usual stuff in a job interview, the plant managers asked my dad [Alan Tiffany] if he had a degree in social work. My dad said no, but if they wanted him to get one,

170

he would be willing. They immediately said, "No, no, that's not necessary", but gave no explanation of why they asked that question. After my dad had worked at the Firthcliffe plant for a couple years, he found out the previous plant engineer had had a degree in social work [as well as engineering], and was a Communist Party member attempting to start a union at the Firthcliffe plant. Well, there had been a big strike, which was broken by the management, and the social worker was run out of town. Anyway, needless to say, my dad never got a degree in social work!

FRED BOOTH DIES

Active for 50 Years in Carpet Plant at Cornwall, N.Y.

Special to THE NEW YORK TIMES

CORNWALL, N.Y., Jan 7. — Fred Booth, chairman of the board directors and treasurer of the Firth Carpet Company, with which he had been associated in various capacities for fifty years, died suddenly at his office yesterday in his seventy-fourth year.

Mr. Booth, who was born in Lightcliff, England, was engaged in the carpet manufacturing business there before he came to Cornwall in 1884 to start the Firth Carpet Company's Firthcliff mill, near here. He remained with the organization until his death.

He was a trustee and director of the New York Military Academy at Cornwall, a director of the Highlands-Quassaick Bank of Newburgh and a life trustee of the Institute of Carpet Manufacturers of America, He was warden of St. John's Episcopal Church.

Survivors are his widow, Mrs Lydia Hirst Booth; two daughters Mrs James H. Patrick and Miss Miriam R. Booth of Cornwall, and a son Francis E. Booth of Boston.

The funeral will be held at 2 o'clock on Tuesday afternoon at St John's Episcopal Church. Burial will be at the convenience of the family in Woodlawn Cemetery Newburgh.

The New York Times

Published January 8, 1934

May 6, 1937: The airship Hindenburg explodes and crashes during its landing at Lakehurst, New Jersey, on the first flight of the 1937 season. The landings of the German airship on American soil would prove to be the last remnant of civility between America and Hitler's Germany.

January 1939: 350 people attend ceremony celebrating Firth Carpet setting a new safety record. Certificate of Merit awarded to Firth Carpet.

1940: France falls to the Germans; 332,226 trapped French,
Dutch, Belgian, and Polish troops are rescued from Dunkirk;
Britain is under attack by the German Air Force

Pictures on right:
The O&W's "streamstyled" Mountaineer at Weehawken and North Bergen on May 28th, 1938
American railroads were trying to lure back passengers and uplift depression-weary spirits with their modern streamlined trains. The O&W, fresh into bankruptcy, could not afford a whole new, all modern streamliner. So veteran #405, and the road's best passenger car stock, were given an in house, top to bottom makeover. With her chrome stack bands and handrails, and a fresh maroon paintjob, the new "Mountaineer" proved to be a real head turner and morale builder. A showpiece of railroad management and employee pride, even as war clouds draw closer to home.

Photos: Ed Crist Collection

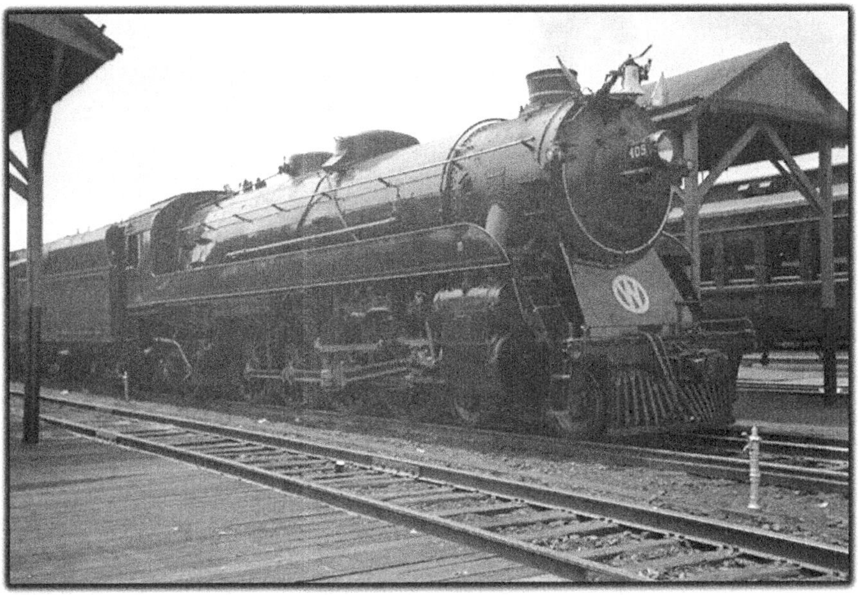

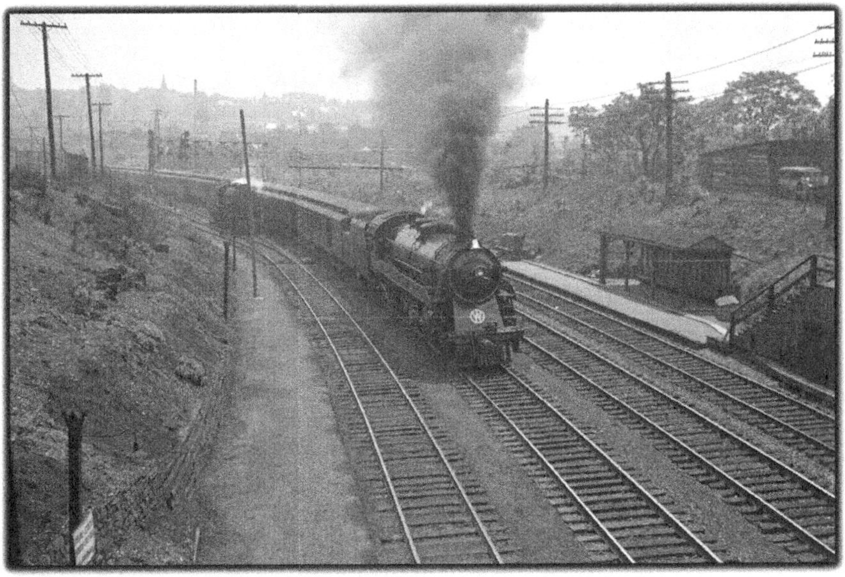

405 rolls by Meadowbrook station, and is about to duck under the Rt. 45 (today Rt. 94) bridge. Barely visible in this photo, the train is passing under the "telltale"- ropes hung from a pole and over the tracks, warning any train crew that might be walking on top of the cars, of low clearance ahead.

Walter Kierzkowski

Orrs Mills, with the station in the top photo (arrow) and with the station already gone, making it the 1920's or later. Note the people standing on the trestle to the right

(Online search)

That last sweet summer of peace: July, 1941

In July of 1941 Mill Street was detoured around the mill and the hollow

In October the Local would carry an ironic headline: "What does 1942 hold in store for you?"

In the days leading up to that fateful December 7th Cornwall was suffering through a water shortage, one that threatened to temporarily shut down Firth Carpet.

Chapter Ten:
World War Two

Firth Safety Record: In November of 1942 the Blending department received a safety award for one quarter million man hours without an accident. The wartime Honor Roll in the background to the right.

NEW YORK, ONTARIO AND WESTERN RAILWAY Frederick Lyford, Trustee

Middletown, N. Y. (GENERAL ORDER N0 405)

December 22, 1941

ALL EMPLOYEES:

We are confronted with a situation, the magnitude and bitterness of which has not heretofore been experienced by the people of this country, and it unfortunately continues to spread its devastating passage over our land.

Each New York, Ontario and Western Railway employee has a personal responsibility in aiding this Railway to properly meet and overcome this attack on our country and its accompanying destruction of life and property by subversive sabotage.

We ask you to not talk with strangers relative to the physical characteristics of any part of this railroad, its train movements of supplies and troops and industrial activities along the line, nor to engage in conversation about these things with any one in places where the conversation may be heard by others.

In other words, we desire to form a New York, Ontario and. Western

employee's Secret Service which shall be so tight that no information

regarding N. Y. 0. & W. activities can be obtained anywhere except at

headquarters,

W. A. Wood O&WRHS collection

January, 1942: Firth claims to be first to fly service flag

March 16, 1942: Firth Carpet secures large contract from U.S.

Army, U.S. Navy and Canadian Governments. Full production by Mid-summer is planned.

February 11, 1943: Closing of Firth's CREX plant in Newburgh means more work in Firthcliffe

February, 11, 1943: Firth has perfected a flexible stretcher; orders coming from Red Cross and civilian defense organizations

Hidden Hazards
"Victory in battle often hinges on crews of Army Engineers who must
clear out deadly land mines ad booby traps before our troops can move
forward. To locate these hidden hazards an electrical device is used to give out a warning tone when a mine is near. Unfortunately this equipment does not detect mines with wooden cases and operating parts. Yet that does not stop the Army in their efforts to find these destruction makers ....they have trained dogs to locate them by scent!
Locating hidden hazards to prevent accidents is equally as important
on the Production Front and we should be as equally determined. Each one of us should be alert for unsafe methods or workplace conditions. When such a condition is located it should be reported promptly for correction!"
From Firth Newsletter, September, 1944
Cornwall Historical Society

February 3, 1944: Bond rally; March: Fire in Carding Department
causes 5,000 dollars in damages;
April: Employee vacations are reinstated as War crisis easing, demands for war materials slowing;

September: Bowling matches to benefit serviceman's Christmas fund
June 6th, 1944: D-Day: The liberation of Europe begins as Allied forces storm the beaches at Normandy

December, 1945: 83 out of 525 of Firth's employees out with influenza

Below and left: Same location, two different worlds
An Erie freight rolls through Hale Eddy in August of 1941, four months before the attack on Pearl Harbor
Next page: Hale Eddy in August of 1942: It's been eight months since President Roosevelt vowed "We will gain the inevitable triumph, So help us God!" By the first summer of the war there were signs that the Axis machine was beginning to crack. Then In August of 1942 came the battles of Stalingrad, North Africa, and Guadalcanal.
The tide of the most destructive war in history was about to turn.

Both photos from Ed Crist's collection/my albums

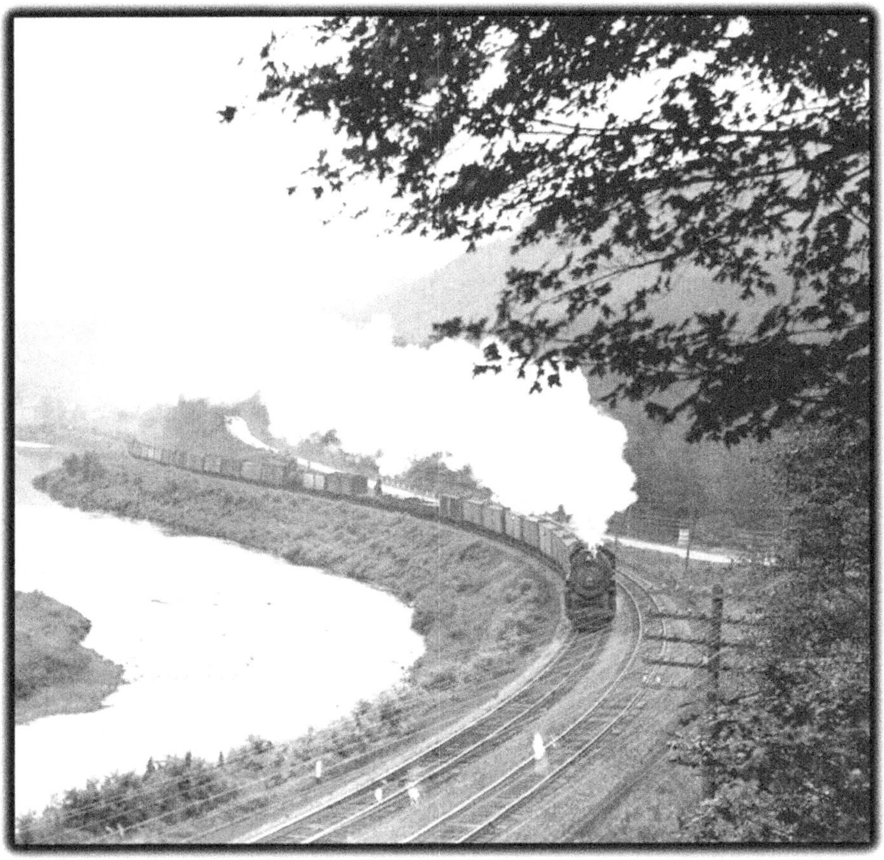

"Good evening, Mr. President. I heard you just had a conference with Winston Churchill on a battleship about war strategy. War strategy, meaning, "Where will we attack the enemy and how are we going to keep Eleanor out of the crossfire?"

"One soldier went to the Hollywood canteen and danced with Hedy Lamarr, Betty Grable and Lana Turner. . . . I don't know if it affected him or not but he was a little late getting back to camp. . . . It was Tuesday before an antiaircraft unit in San Diego could shoot him down." Bob Hope

April 1945 would see the Allies finally able to liberate the last of the Nazi Concentration camps. At the same time, Roosevelt was preparing his Jefferson Day Speech, finishing with "Let us move forward with a strong and active faith".

It was the last speech he would ever write before a stroke ended the life of the man who lived a private hell that only those that have been through it could fathom; and then taught a crippled nation how to walk again.

> *"Oh! Hand me down my walking cane*
> *Hand me down my walking cane*
> *Hand me down my walking cane*
> *I'm gonna leave on the midnight train*
> *'Cause all my cares been taken away*
> *If I had listed to what momma said*
> *If I had listen to what momma said*
> *If I had listened to what momma said*
> *I'd be sleeping in a feather bed*
> *'Cause all my cares been taken away"*

The Times wrote the next day: "In home communities -- Brooklyn, the Bronx, Harlem, Queens -- women left their dinners on the stoves to stand in neighborhood groups, passing the word, or discussing it with bated breath. Groups, small at first and ever-growing, assembled in silence wherever a shopkeeper had turned his radio speaker toward the street."

Yank Magazine, read by soldiers and sailors throughout the world, reported: "Nowhere was grief so open as in the poorest neighborhoods of New York. In Old St. Patrick's in the heart of the Italian district on the lower east side, bowed, shabby figures came and went and, by the day after the President died, hundreds of candles burned in front of the altar. 'Never,' said a priest, 'have so many candles burned in this church.'

In that first week of June in 1944 the sun would shine, as it always has
But the world was in darkness, as dark as it had ever been in history
An evil hand threatened to take away the light of freedom
We can never comprehend how such evil can exist in the world
Nor can we comprehend how God, in his almighty powers, created enough love, honor, and courage to drive the men he would send to rescue freedom from evil.
We call them heroes
They do not call themselves heroes
These were scared lads, eighteen years old, nineteen years old; twenty years old
Some had lied about their age to join the fight
They all knew that they might not survive the wall of gun fire that they were about to march into
But with a love greater than self they all went
They came from every walk of life
From every nationality
They came together, to cross a stormy sea
To land on beaches where gunfire and screams pierced the air
And all that was death lay in wait at the top of the cliffs
The beaches would quickly be covered in carnage
But our sons, pride of our nation, kept crossing those beaches, and climbed those cliffs
Where gunfire and screams pierced the air
Many fell
Sons, brothers, fiancés, kept coming
Many more would fall
But a continent was finally saved
Time passes
We look upon those beaches that are so peaceful now
It's so easy to forget a time when gunfire and screams pierced the air
It's so easy to ignore the ghosts that linger here
With every passing year, more of the men that fought the most destructive war in history rejoin their comrades that will forever be eighteen, nineteen and twenty

They pray to us that we never forget

In God's name, we must never forget

Bob McCue

CARPET FIRTH COMPANY
295 FIFTH AVENUE, NEW YORK CITY

OFFICE OF THE PRESIDENT

December 20, 1945

To the Employees,
Firth Carpet Company,
Firthcliffe, N. Y.

Dear Friends:—

We celebrate our first peacetime Holiday in four years. That, in itself, makes it a day of major importance— exceeded only by the Spirit of Christmas which we have held to and cherished through all the ominous years. It has been a "refuge and strength" in our hours of need.

Against the somber past the future opens bright and fair with happy prospects. Man and his handiwork shall turn to the ways of peace and we will pursue our American privileges so dearly won, with the reverence and appreciation such a great blessing so well deserves.

We are still convalescent in our minds and hearts, proud in our victory and dedicated to sustaining it. We won't forget the depreciation of real values which cost us so dearly in the past but will, rather, hold precious the worthwhile things in life — brotherly love and the fulfilment of its true purpose will be our principal consideration.

I send you my heartiest and festive greetings in the above mood and join you in sharing that precious thing "Peace on Earth" which we now have and "Good Will to Men" which we will practice.

Yours most cordially,

HAROLD E. WADLEY

HEW/d

Above and next two pages: World War Two Memorial that
originally stood in front of the Firthcliffe Clubhouse
The memorial was dedicated on May 4th, 1946 and sponsored
by the Firthcliffe Army-Navy Club with Samuel Docherty
Chairman and assisted by Mrs. Margaret Mosher, club
President; Mrs. Malvin Brown and Mrs.
Calvin Smith. The NYMA band played at the dedication
ceremony.

The monument now stands by Rings Pond.
Cornwall Local/Cornwall Public Library

Pictures of the Dedication

Monument Dedication-Firth Newsletter
John Arnott-George Kane

THIS STONE
TAKEN FROM A SPOT 12 MILES
THE NORMANDY BEACHHEAD AND
OF THE MEN AND WOMEN OF WRECLESFIELD
WHO SERVED THEIR COUNTRY
IN WORLD WAR II AND AS
AN ENDURING TRIBUTE
TO THOSE WHO GAVE THE
LAST FULL MEASURE OF DEVOTION
NOVEMBER 1945

God bless America, land that I love,
Stand beside her and guide her
Through the night with a light from above

From the mountains, to the prairies,
To the oceans white with foam,
God bless America,
My home sweet home

Jan 24, 1946: Sales at
Firth Carpet over 6 million,
over
4.8 million in 1944

March: Old water
wheels removed

CHS 1926 "Best spellers in Grade 5"
William Yearwood

Eleanor Richardson

Evelyn Van Duzer

Violet Cutler

Alfred Prause

Credit to JoAnn Paige

Chapter Eleven:
Postwar Years
Growing up in Firthcliffe
By Ed Smith

The Firth club: This was a hot spot in Firthcliffe, my father Edwin Smith was a pin boy in the bowling alley which was downstairs when he was 15 or so, I am sure that is now about 100 years ago. In the clubhouse on the left was Bob Smith, who was the barber. I had my first haircut there and it was all of 25 cents which was a lot of money back then.

The outside of the club was always kept so nice by Dave Stevenson. There was a flag pole and a bed of flowers that was always kept nice.

Directly across the hall from the barber shop was the post office. My uncle, Uncle Jim Baron, was the postmaster and my mother worked there as a clerk when she was 16 or so. The post office had brass boxes and combinations and that was how we all got our mail. People would sit in wood rocking chairs at the clubhouse and that was a meeting place for most. Then the post office moved to its present location on Main Street. At that time, Mr. Mc Tammaney was the postmaster and he lived up by the old ball lot.

When you went downstairs to the canteen where the bowling alley was you could buy soda and things like that from a little concession. I don't know who ran it.

Christmas at the Firthcliffe Club House: The parents were expected to buy the gift and they would put it under the tree on the stage. We would all line up and Santa would let us sit on his lap, photograph and give us our gift. We also each got a box of hard cinnamon and green colored Christmas candy. The box had a string on it.

In years to come they changed it with a stocking that was made from red twine. After the Christmas party we would all sing Christmas carols and someone played the piano.

I remember the back, the outside of the club house had a metal fire escape that pointed towards Frost Lane, glad we never had to use it, it didn't look safe even way back then! *1
Even though they built the bowling alley on route 9W near the old state trooper barracks there were people who still used the bowling alley at the Firth club. It was always so terribly hot and we had no A C back then.
Behind the Firth club house the area was lower than most. If you think about it, all the homes on Willow Ave had their septic tanks and that water flowed toward the low part of that area behind the club house. It always smelled like a sewer and there were mosquitoes galore.*2

Everyone knew the Firth carpet company just as the mill, no other name needed, and the lot at the top of Algernon was just referred to as either the field or the ball field.
The Firths had many family events for the workers, during the summer they would host clam bakes and picnics with races and soft ball games. Under the trees were picnic tables and as I recall for some reason they had one water pipe for running water.
The bus in Firthcliffe: Jimmy Brunton was one of the drivers and was married to Anne Brunton. Jimmy was a cripple. The evening bus would come to Firthcliffe at exactly 8:20PM. My grandmother and I used to wait in the dining room and wait for it to come over the hill. She called it the "light that never fails". When we saw the bus she would hurry to get supper ready for my grandfather.

1 Firthcliffe Club would survive a fire on December 4, 1951, only to be gutted in a fire on the morning of October 23, 1970.
2 It was this growing concern over the sewers that would cause Cornwall to incorporate a separate sewer district for Firthcliffe in the 1960's.

He would park the bus at the corner of Willow Ave and Frost Lane which was not really very safe for anyone coming over the hill and down towards the Firth club. He would come in, eat supper and leave at 8:55 PM, the last bus to Newburgh was at 9 PM, he would go to the Firth club, turn around and start the route. I remember one night the emergency brake did not hold or he did not have it in gear and the bus let loose on the hill, It ran into the fire hydrant right in front of Chippy Halstead's home and snapped it off. Halstead's home was on the corner of Frost Lane and Willow Avenue,

When the mill was in full swing, the bus would go down the hill at Mill Street and turn around by the timekeepers building, people would get on the bus to go home after working.

There was a building on the right when you drove down the street towards the mill. It housed the time cards and had a guard. When the whistle blew the one shift would come out, the other in and they passed through this time building. When I was little I went to the mill one time and saw the looms and the shuttles going back and forth, very noisy, the weavers had to watch the looms and had a pair of shears, there were huge wood spools for the thread.

The Firth mill had a whistle to sound to end the shift but if it blew in between it meant trouble. I recall it going off when the creek flooded following a severe rain storm and flooding the weaving section. I remember a fire one time. You could hear the high pitched whistle, so unlike the fire horn from quite a distance. When that sounded you would see the people leave their homes and head towards the mill. It really was the center of town and we all depended on it.

Jim Barton was the postmaster in Firthcliffe until they closed it and moved to Main Street. His wife Annie was my grand-mother's sister and she worked for Firth Carpet until she retired many years after he had died. My father worked there, he was a weaver. Annie worked in the finishing room.

Before the A&P and the Grand Union- this would be in the 1940's and before- there were two stores, one in Cornwall near the blind home and another on the hill going down Mill St. Both of the owners were my uncles. Bill Weeks and his wife Libby owned the store on Main Street, not far from the blind home. That was the main grocery store for Cornwall. Uncle Bill Weeks was an entrepreneur and even had home deliveries. My Uncle Bill Babcock owned the other store on Mill Street, just up from Anna Smith's store.

(Above) Post Office and Anna's store, just up the hill from the mill and station- Sometime after the Post Office moved into the Firthcliffe club, Anna's store moved over into the Post Office building and remained there for many years, outliving the railroad, the club and the mill itself.

Anna lived next door to the store and would just stay there all the time taking care of her invalid father. She would hear a customer and go to the store. Her specialty for the kids of course was penny candy and an ice cream sandwich she would make with MY DREAM ICE CREAM. I remember when the A& P opened on Main Street in upper Cornwall, the smell of the fresh ground coffee. Then came the Grand Union and that was the beginning of the end of the small grocery stores.

The fire station was next to the Firth Clubhouse. This was closed and the fire station moved to Main Street in Cornwall, for years the building still housed an old horse drawn fire truck, I recall in the cellar of this building was an immense wood bar with alcohol. The fire house was then changed to a beauty salon. On the outside of it they kept the red fire switch you would have to run to ring for the fire dept and of course there was a fire whistle on top of it. The fire whistle blew every night at exactly 5 PM, that was the signal for all children to go home, eat your supper and do whatever, It was just a given that nearly all of us followed. The fire whistle would also ring on 12 noon on Saturdays.
Each resident was given an orange card. It had a series of numbers posted on the left side of it and then to the right was a street marker. For example 7 was mutual aid, it would be coded like 2-2, 2-3, 3-2. You would count the whistles and then look at the fire chart, the orange card, and then you would know about where the fire was, if you were a fireman you just drove to that area and eventually find out what was going on.

Wednesday, July 2, 1975 - Supplement to The Cornwall LOCAL - Page 13

They Fought Against Fires

FIRE DEPARTMENT, Firthcliffe, N. Y.

We had a Holsum bread truck that made deliveries. If you were of means you could use another bread company that was expensive called Dugan.

We had kerosene deliveries from Otto Gauer who lived near the blind home. There were several vegetable trucks that made rounds also.

Behind the Halstead home they had a garden, everyone in fact had gardens back then in their back yards. * They would "put up" the vegetables for the winter months. Many of those homes were mill homes and they all had a garden in the back. My aunt Mary Smith and her husband Calvin lived there, she worked in the mill as almost everyone else did.

* Around the time of the First World War, Firth Carpet was encouraging their employees to grow gardens by offering to plow their yards at no charge.

An old pick up truck would deliver and sell Adirondack chairs for outside, everyone had to have a pair of these and if you had money, a table for them also. There was the rag man and I forgot his name. The ice man was Slip Everett and he lived in lower Cornwall near Santoro's bar and grill at the circle.

Telephones: In the entire Firthcliffe area there was one pay phone for the general public to use and that was an old wood box one with folding doors in the club house just past the barber shop on the left. It had a seat in it, a fan that turned on when you closed the door and cost 10 cents. That was so much money back then.

To let my parents know that I had got there okay or whatever we had a signal. You would dial the operator and make a person to person collect call so it did not cost any money. When my mother would answer her phone the operator would say: ...."person to person call for John Doe" and her response would be, "Oh, I am sorry he is not here". The phone call did not cost a cent and was the signal that I had got there okay. I am sure the operators all knew this trick that everyone played. I don't think they have person to person calls anymore either.

The next pay phone was located at Black Rock Fish and Game club in Mountainville.

In the town of Cornwall the only phone was at Hazards drug store. There was a pay phone at the new CCHS but that was built in 1957. If we needed the police we had to call the state troopers but I don't really ever remember them being their much. Herb O'dell was the top police officer and well respected, he directed traffic in front of Cornwall High School for years.

In the winter months people would throw their ash from the coal furnaces onto the street to get more traction in the snow and ice, I recall doing that when I was little.

Firthcliffe as well as all the other communities would be invaded by the "gypsies" who came in on old dilapidated pick up trucks. Some were on wagons with horses pulling them. They would go from house to house panhandling and if you did not give them anything they would threaten to put a curse on you or even steal right from under your nose.

When the gypsies came, the phones rang off the hook in Firthcliffe. Every person that had a phone would call the other. Remember, we had party lines and all the people would stay inside and pretend not to be home. I remember that happening for years when I was young.

The railroad trestle had guards protecting it during World War 1 and 2 both. There was a man who was walking the trestle guarding it and fell to his death. He was the son of one of the people that owned Sachs, 5th Avenue.

There was a civil defense yellow sign in the Firthcliffe Club which was designated as an air raid shelter, downstairs in the bowing alley. That was it for the entire town. The air raid signal was one long blast. I remember it going off once and had the entire town in helter-skelter- the switch had stuck!

Firth Newsletter memo *Michael Raab*

FIRTH ANNUAL OUTING

The Firthcliffe Club Committee has plans well underway for our Annual Outing, August 10th, with a rain date of August 17th.

A bulletin of events will be posted in the various departments at a later date. We have again chosen our own Firth Recreation Field for the event because of its ideal location.

Our 30 foot swimming pool will again be installed for the occasion, and we have contracted for the "Diesel" train which was very popular with the youngsters last year.

Our 1956 Outing was one of our best in attendance and we are looking forward to a big turnout this year. We will have Hot Dogs, Hamburgers, Soda-pop and Ice Cream as usual, but suggest that you bring the family picnic basket and spend the day in a social visit with old friends in the plant and in the community.

THE PERSONNEL OFFICE

Next two pages: Firth's delivery trucks

Doug Spaulding Collection

THURSDAY, DECEMBER 30, 1948

Firth Announces Producton Of New Type Carpet

(Continued from Page 1)

scientists, technicians and stylists for the past five years, "Cellini", Mr. Wadely stated "attains an objective with which manufacturers have sought for years — production of a combination of high and low pile yarn on an Axminster loom, with an effect similar to the so-called low wire background of the Wilton process.

So-called carved carpet has been produced for years as Chenille, the lush, heavy pile, semi-tailored carpet, which is later hand sheared or "carved" to create the design. A comparable effect has been obtained in recent years on Wilton looms, Mrs. Wadley explained.

Previous attempts to produce high style, carved effect carpet by the Axminster process have not been too successful. One employed a combination of sharply twisted and straight yarns, and twisted yarns sinking below the level of the straight yarn to give the two level effect. However, the twist has a tendency to unravel and to rise above the surface of the high yarn, destroying the pattern. Another styling used the principle of leaving out threads at intervals to outline the pattern. This method also falls short of attaining a true carved effect.

The new product is woven in two patterns, both suggested by designs of the 16th century sculptor, Benvenuto Cellini. One is inspired by the delicate carvings and tracery in mother-of-pearl and silver basin, long a part of the Imperial Austrian Treasury. The second is an adaptation from the design motifs on the famous Cellini cup in the New York Metropolitan Museum, according to President Wadley.

5 Years in Development

Under development for the past five years, the first "Cellini" took finisher from two years ago after undergoing rigid tests. For the past couple of years several "Cellini" carpets have been used in the homes of Firth officials to prove the wearability under normal conditions.

Mr. Wadley stated that the new carpet is now in production and will begin going out in increasing volume to distributors early next month. Distribution will be allocated for some months. Retail prices will be $11 to $12 a yard, according to shipping charges. It will be first produced in silver, harvest beige, limoges rose and pine wood green.

This new product was produced at the Firthcliffe plant under the direction of General Manager Russell R. Matthews.

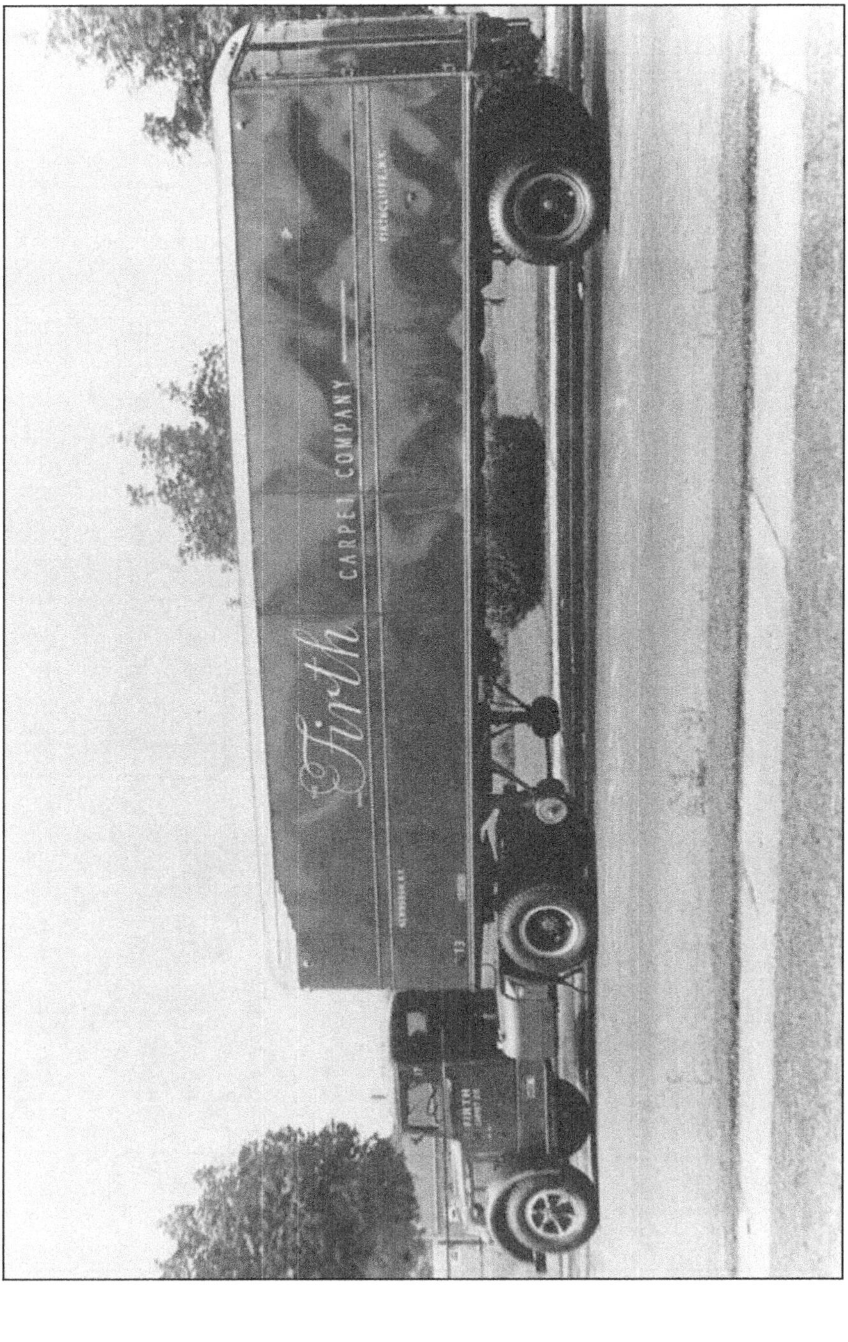
Firth
CARPET COMPANY

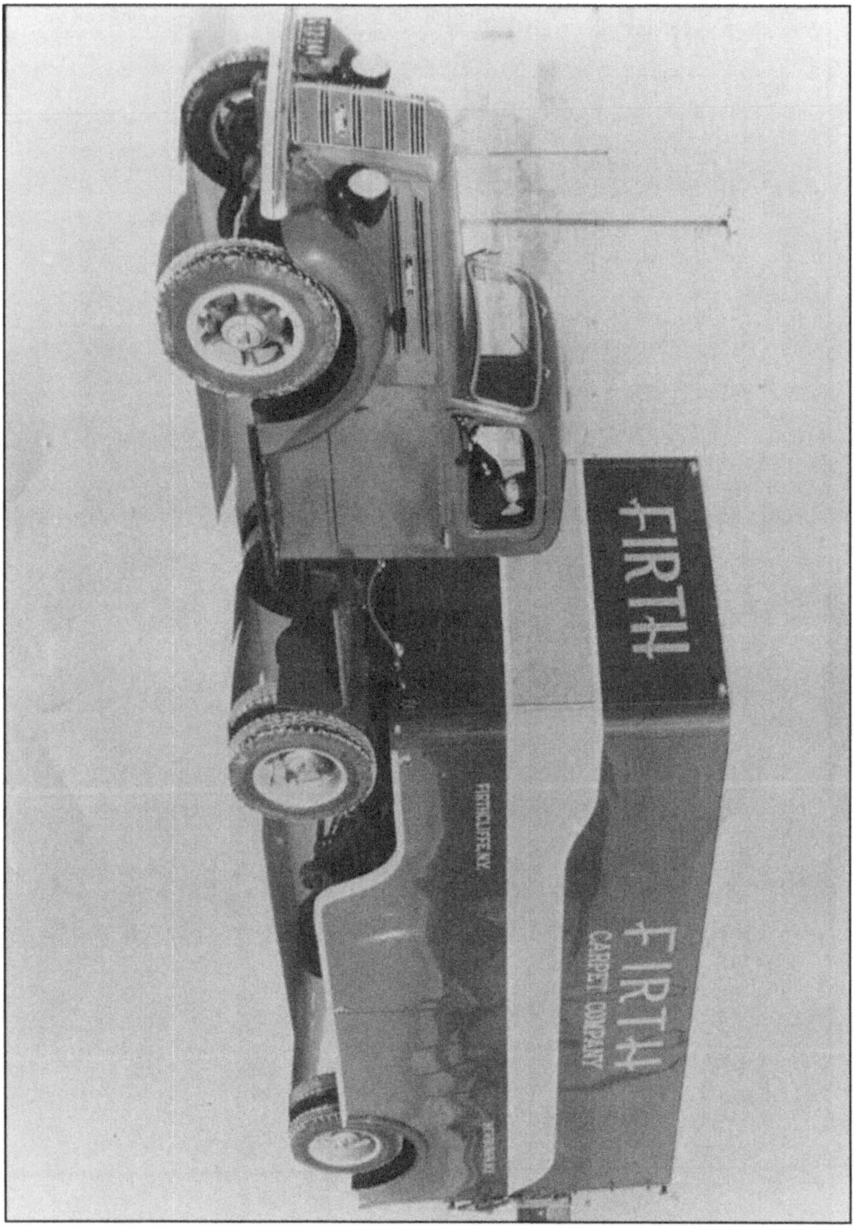
FIRTH
FIRTH
CARPET COMPANY

Chapter Twelve:
A hammer built the railroad, a gavel closes it….

Possibly Guy Twaddel's last run
Guy worked for the Railroad for over 40 years,
and was on one of the last runs through
Middletown in 1957.

Ed Crist albums/my collection

O&WRHS

After passenger service on the O&W ended in September of 1953, Firthcliffe station would remain open with a station agent* to serve the carpet company and for customers such as Ushman's Lumber in Cornwall.

Harry Quick was the stationmaster at Firthcliffe from1943 to the early 1950's. His daughter, Phyllis Quick Merrill was stationmaster from the early 50's until the station closed. "My time and place with the O&W Railway", Jim Parella; O&W Observer: O&W's - Middletown branch by Doug Barberio, 2008

When the railroad closed in March of 1957, an eviction order was sent to all the stations that still had agents living in them as all buildings on railroad property were about to be boarded up. *O&WRHS archives*

Memorial Prayer
Presented at the 50th anniversary program of the closing of the O&W Railroad, held at M&NJ Railroad Station at Middletown, N.Y.
By Rev. Daniel Hulseapple

"Almighty and Everlasting God, by whose grace and mercy all things were made, by whom mankind was created and made to live through the gift of the breath of life: before you, O God of All, we come with humble hearts and souls. Through the ages, you have endowed your creation with skills and understanding which have enabled the life which first you bestowed to endure and to continue. By your mercy, and with your blessing, you have imparted to us ever increasing knowledge so that we could use the ordering of your universe to make our dwelling time upon this earth a time in which to rejoice and be thankful.

This place in which we gather is such a place from a time not so far back in our past, a time when the power of steam was harnessed to produce the energy of mighty machines whose purpose was to make our lives easier and more productive. We gather here, to remember those from the past, who lives were dedicated to this industry of railroading. As pioneers, they sometimes gave their lives in the development of trails and paths into roadways for these mighty giants, which by your blessing, were created by humans hands. We are here to thank you for the ingenuity of the skills of the craftsmen who built these wonders; we are here to thank you for those who had the ability to drive these marvels, enabling their power to be used for the good of all; we are here to thank you for those whose talents kept these "iron horses" in good repair.

But we remember not only those of the past, but also those who yet today labor in this field, continuing to create and maintain these systems for the movement of goods and peoples from place to place. Only through their unfaltering pursuits of service for others do we share in the pleasure of using these great conveyors of products and people. Grant to those who have departed this physical world their rewards for faithfulness to you through their talents; keep faithful those who now strive to continue in service with the same fervor as those men and women from days of old; and bless all those who are yet to be, who, in their own time and place, will strive to keep alive that spirit of service to others in providing and maintaining the means of convenient travel along the rails of life.

Here, O God, in this place, and in this time, we raise up our memories of friends and family who have serve you well, and thank you for the opportunity in sharing life with them. And when that day comes for each of us to stand in your presence beyond this earthly life, may we receive a kindred welcome, and a fond remembrance, by those we leave behind.

To you O God, Creator and Sustainer of all life, be the glory, for ever and ever. Amen".

Reverend Hulseapple's father was an O&W employee

1946: Northbound train #1 climbs the grade out of Cornwall and is approaching Firthcliffe. It is only two more years before that last steam engine runs on the O&W. And Only a decade remains before the familiar sounds of a train echoing off the hills will vanish from the Firthcliffe landscape forever.
Bob Collins photo/O&WRHS

Crossing Mill Street, and is about to roll over the Orrs
Mills bridge 300 feet ahead.
Older photo: O&WRHS

Orrs Mills trestle" Then and now..

Page 215: An Erie freight rolls across the
O&W mainline at Campbell Hall station
The date is March 28th, 1957

The N.Y. Ontario and Western Railroad-
the legendary "Old and Weary"-
has one day left to live.

Jim Shaugnessy photo, Ed Crist albums/my collection

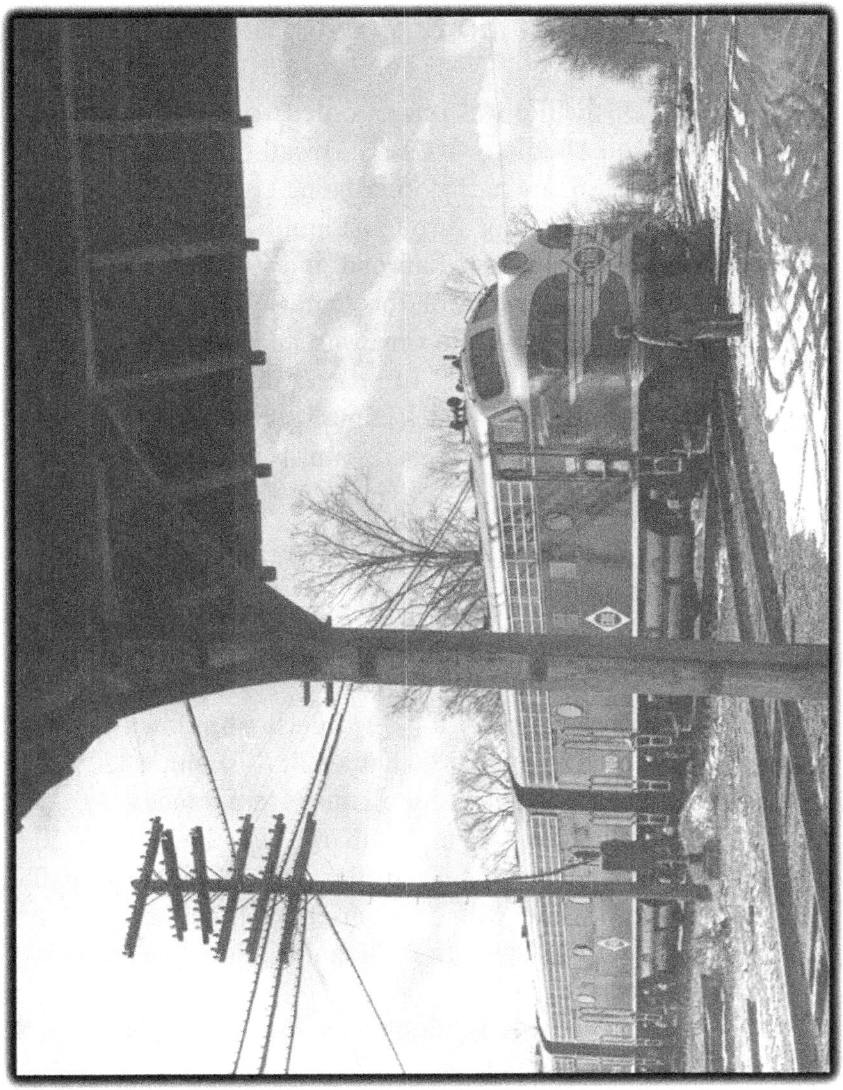

Next four pages: The demise of the New York, Ontario & Western Railroad

By 1949 Firthcliffe was one of only two stations* on the line between Middletown and Cornwall that had not been sold off or torn down, the other being Campbell Hall. The freight traffic coming through Campbell Hall from the connecting New Haven Railroad and its Maybrook yard was now the mainstay of the Ontario's income. While anything further south to Cornwall and Weehawken was a single daily freight in each direction. Modern improvements like Diesel locomotives helped the O&W fight the good fight right up until its court ordered shutdown in 1957.

Will Embargo All Shipments
Middletown Times Herald, March, 1957

Plans are underway for an orderly shutdown of the O&W Railroad by March 29 James B. Kilsheimer III, one of the road's receivers told the Times Herald today.

Mr. Kilsheimer said an embargo will be put on all O&W shipments so that no traffic will be accepted and all goods on the line will be cleared by the closing date ordered by Judge Sylvester P. Ryan. No date has been set by the embargo.

The receivers will accumulate as much as much of the railroad's equipment as possible, including diesels, cabooses, tankers and other cars in Middletown for custodial care. They want to have everything together when the system is sold, in pieces or in its entirety, Mr. Kilsheimer said.

The proceeds of the sale, when it develops, will be used to repay persons who contributed to the special fun raising drive last month. The amount amounted to more than $227,000, the receiver reported. He said it will take weeks or months before it can be repaid, depending on how long it takes the U.S. government to clear its suit against the road.

Meanwhile, in Middletown, efforts are underway to gain aid for shippers and receivers using the O&W's facilities.

Mayor Raymond E. Swalm has acquired a list of carload shippers from Middletown to Cadosia in Delaware County. He said he will make copies of the list to send to the State Department of Commerce, the Erie Railroad, Congressman Katherine St. George and to the Interstate Commerce Commission, asking them to do all they can to ensure the shippers of this area they will not be left without adequate facilities to transport their goods. He will urge the Erie to take over the shipments when the O&W ceases to operate.

Judge Ryan ordered the railroad, which has been in bankruptcy for 30 years, to cease operations on March 29th. "I'm sorry", said Ryan, "we can't operate because we want to. We don't have the money or the time". The Judge said, however, that he hoped to sell the railroad as an entity and not as "junk." Last November, a Boston firm of railroad operators offered $4.000.000 for the road.

Mr. Kilsheimer told the court that despite economies of more than $70.000 a month, a "substantial loss of freight traffic has raised a critical situation." "Our best estimate", Mr. Kilsheimer said, "Is that this railroad can operate to March 29th, at which time it appears that there will be insufficient cash."

For many months the O&W has been given new leases on life by federal authorities in the hope that it could become a growing concern. The receivers laid off more than 200 employees to cut down costs, but the road still has been losing $135,000 a month.

Last Tuesday in the nation's capital, the receivers conferred with the Justice Department, which has a seven-million dollar back tax lien against the railroad; with the Treasury Department, and both Senators from New York.

Additional funds were not available, and the Department of Defense said that the line did not qualify as necessary to the national defense. Although several neighboring carriers have expressed interest in bidding for portions of the railroad, or even the entire system, Kilsheimer said nothing could be consummated until after the road halted operations, two weeks from tonight.

O&W Calls it quits
By Saul Freilich

The jobs of 450 persons were wiped out last night when the 80 year old New York, Ontario and Western Railroad officially ceased operations. Sixty-six others will remain at their posts until they are dismissed. The last scheduled train arrived in Middletown at 5P.M. yesterday though two other unscheduled trains followed. The last one came from Oswego and arrived at 3:15 A.M. today.

Following the shutdown, plans wee underway to begin the final accounting and inventory of equipment owned by the defunct road. Robert McGraw, general manager, said that he will remain at work until the O&W is completely liquidated to supervise the inventory and final disposal of property.

Harry Weeks, office manager, reported today that 30 persons would be retained in the accounting office in Middletown and six office employees in New York would remain. Other employees who will be retained on the payroll include watchmen along the line.

Brave, futile fight to save "Old and Weary" from death
By Robert Farrington

New York (AP)-The New York, Ontario and Western died at midnight last night at the age of 80 after a lingering bankruptcy.

The cause of death: Her income couldn't catch up with her outgo. Right to the end the mourners though that the railroad would recover and sit up. At the bedside was as staggering an array of creditors as any 541 mile line ever had. Bigger railroads would have gulped at her 100 million dollar pile of debts. She fought to the end and her creditors and friends fought beside her. The New York State Civil Defense Commission yesterday reaffirmed its previous ruling that the road is not essential to civil defense. Gov Harriman had signed a special bill designed to enable the commission to operate the road. Even as late as last night 10 Republican members of the state Legislature sent a telegram to the commission asking it to take over the line "in accord with the mandate of the people" and the Legislature. The lawmakers who sent the telegram represent counties along the O&W route.

She was unique for the affection and loyalty she inspired. No road ever put up a more valiant struggle against adversity.

They'll sell the locomotives and some of her tracks and the station to other railroads and what can't be sold will be scrapped. Yet she'll be remembered. She will be remembered by the college students, gray haired old men now who rode her creeping midnight milk trains in the long ago and dubbed her the "Old and Weary" and the "Out and Walk". She'll be remembered by the tens of thousands who laughed and sang on her coaches to Catskill resorts thirty years ago.

Ten percent more business, six months more time might have saved her, said Federal Judge Sylvester J. Ryan.

The same regretful cry echoes back through the record of her bankrupt years.

Abridged version of larger article
END

Farrington's column put a sentimental twist on an event whose impact on the local economy we are still feeling today. She was the first railroad to fall and sadly, was far from the last. William Helmer, with his book "The long life and slow death of the O&W", finishes his eulogy for the O&W and its era with "...........When the far off whistle made dreamers of us all."

Washer from the Orrs Mills trestle
Author's collection

That dreary day in 1957 was a sad and far cry from that (now long forgotten) day in 1873, when the last spike was driven of the New York and Oswego Midland RR (Later the Ontario and Western). That day back in 1873 is explained here in a 1967 article in the Walton Herald:

First Gasps of the O & W Described in Article

The Norwich Evening Sun of Aug. 8 carries a story by Alice C. Muller concerning the driving of the last spike for construction of the New York Oswego Midland Railroad.

Excerpts from her article follow:

The driving of the last spike on a railroad was usually accompanied by solemn ceremony and great jubilation. It marked the end of the troublesome period of construction and beginning of the hopeful years of operation.

Early railroads never came easy. The New York Oswego Midland Railroad, later known as the New York Ontario and Western Railway, had more than its share of adversity from the time it was incorporated on Jan. 11, 1866 until the day it ceased to operate on March 29, 1957.

In spite of every adversity, the Herculean task of building a railroad over one of the most difficult routes in New York state was accomplished and the day for celebrating the fact arrived.

The following account was published in 1873 and it gives a graphic description of the dedication of the railroad.

A Crowning Event

"A dispatch was received stating that before July 9, 1873, drifted away the last spike would be driven. Before noon an excursion was under way to witness the crowning event. The hour of departure was announced to be 12:45 p. m. By this time the excursionists numbered about 100 from Norwich. (There is no doubt that this excursion started at Oswego at an earlier hour.)

Some packed quick lunches and others, in their haste, forgot to. Many left with their noon hour lunch. Two passenger coaches left Norwich and a few passengers were added at Oxford. The coaches were drawn by the 'Delaware,' No. 4, and Emory Card was the engineer. This was a free ride.

The Sidney Centre Bridge.

The train proceeded over Lyon Brook bridge, stopped at Oxford, then on to Sidney Centre, 800 feet of the way on a wooden trestle ninety feet high and 1408 feet of the way on a magnificent bridge built after the plan of the Lyon Brook bridge, and rising 104 feet above Carr's Creek, which flowed beneath.

A few miles beyond the next station, Merrickville, they encountered the Zig-Zag's switch back, an engineering contrivance to scale Hard Scrabble (Northfield) mountain. About three miles are traveled here to advance three-quarters of a mile.

At Walton the Brass Band joined the excursion. At this point the excursionists changed to open flat cars. Then began a scramble for seats, planks, chunks of wood and old boxes to sit on. Some grew faint hearted at this point and remained at Walton. Those riding on the first cars were showered with cinders. Some clothes showed marks of hot cinders as long as they were clothes.

Leaving Hancock they came to a tunnel 1,200 feet long which pierced Hawk Mountain. In the midst of profound darkness, the passengers almost suffocated from smoke pouring out of the engine.

Very suddenly the warm sunny day grew cold and caught most of the passengers with no coats. It was a chilly ride on through

Park's Eddy, Trout Brook, Pull Hair, James Cut, Whirling Eddy, and so on until they came to Hell Hole, a point 12 miles west of Westfield.

Here the smoke of the New York excursion train came into view and the train halted. The group disembarked and hastened to the point where the connection was to be made. A rail twelve feet long was all that was needed. On it was cut the name, 'D. C. Littlejohn.' It was the last rail of the eastern section was named 'Opdyke.' The moment had now come for the driving of the last spike. Dr. Henry Bartlett was elected chairman of the meeting and he called upon Elisha P. Wheeler of Middletown, ex-Vice President of the road to drive the spike. The spike had been brought from Norwich. Someone said, 'Drive it good!' Then the only sound heard was the blow of the hammer as the white-haired man drove the spike home, striking the last blow at 8:15. When the deed was done, a cannon which had been brought up from Ellenville, spoke. Five locomotive whistles screamed and the band played Gen. Chamberlin's march. When the noise ceased, he broke a bottle of wine and poured it over the last rail.

About nine o'clock the Norwich men began to return. The air grew colder and damp. No one had anything to say. All was white with snow. Men huddled together back to back and crowded to keep warm. The mercury of their depressed spirits sunk lowest in the thermometer of their distress as the train halted at a water tank 8 miles from Walton. There was still eight miles to go on lank stomachs and in bitter cold. The stoutest hearts quailed.

At Walton they were met with cheers and fed. Then all the party boarded the coaches and they arrived back at Norwich at 4:45."

Ed Crist albums/my collection

217

Abandoned O&W "hacks"
Camp Shanks, Orangeburg NY
Stored and scrapped there

Ed Crist albums/my collection

Chapter Thirteen:
Firth Carpet in the last years

FIRTH'S SUCCESS

Last week's announcement of a nine-and-a-half cents per hour pay raise by Firth Carpet Company was very good news to the hundreds of employees who will benefit by it.

For more than twenty years the Firth Company has been outstanding for its enlightened and pleasant employee-management relations. The beneficial results of this era of good feeling have been apparent in Cornwall and throughout a wide area in the county where Firth workers have their homes. Prosperity seems to bring a personal feeling of well-being and satisfaction that is reflected in a man's attitude toward his community.

The peaceful industrial and labor relations that have been promoted by voluntary agreements between workers and employers at Firth are particularly commendable in a period that has been characterized by unrest and strikes in most of the major industries throughout the country. It is especially notable that Firth's pleasant labor relations have been maintained without the formation of a labor union—an achievement that points to a very intelligent approach and understanding of labor problems on the part of management.

No small share of the credit for the development of fine cooperation between workers and employers in our local plant goes to Russell R. Matthews under whose management Firth workers have enjoyed a long period of security when all their differences have been adjusted, comfortably "within the family".

Other industries would do well to study Firth's success in labor-management relations and find out if their procedures could not be applied elsewhere in the industrial world. The more often disputes between employers and workers can be reconciled without government interference, the longer we are likely to retain our system of free enterprise.

January, 5th, 1950: Firth Club Committee presents television to Firth club.

January, 1951: Report: Firth sets sales record in 1950: up 62% over 1949.

February, 1952: 1000 employees in three shifts, up from 560 six months before.

From the Cornwall Local January of 1954:

A reporter from this newspaper had the opportunity this week to inspect the Firth Carpet Company's new, modern plant hospital, which was recently enlarged and fully equipped to accommodate the new health care program inaugurated at the plant.

When we entered the hospital which is located on the first floor of the spinning mill, we walk into the spacious office and treatment room. We are greeted by Mrs. Marion McDonal, a registered nurse, who was with the Orange County Public Health Nursing Service for the past eight years. She accepted a position at the plant hospital on November 15 and for the past few weeks assisted in setting up the hospital which began to function in its enlarged capacity on December 29th.

We were also greeted by Miss Mollie Quinlan, who has been a member of the plant hospital staff for many years. Mrs. Mary Mitchell, also a longtime member of the staff, serves in the hospital evenings.

Looking over this modern hospital we find a large array of equipment that is used in the examinations and treatment of employees. Just off the main room is a waiting room which is also used as an auxiliary treatment room. Adjoining this room is the examination room, which is well equipped with the necessary implements used in examining the employees.

The health care program was set up under the direction of George R. Dempsey, who is in charge of the hospital and Mrs. Virginia Maneer, nurse consultant for the Liberty Mutual Insurance Co. Dr. Dempsey will be at the plant from 11 to 12 a.m. and from 3:30 to 4:30 p.m. each day except Thursdays to give examinations.

We are told that the basic purpose of the new hospital is to check the health of the employees periodically. They will be examined for structural defects, defective hearing, back injuries, etc., the detection of which might help to prevent an accident.

The personnel of the plant hospital will attempt to keep the employees of the plant in as good as shape as possible, and to acquaint them with good hygiene and health habits through an education program

No treatments will be given, except to those who sustain an injury while at work at the plant.

DR. DEMPSEY — cutting his birthday cake at a little party given him by the Plant Hospital and Personnel Depts.

1955-The caption reads: "Dr. Dempsey-cutting his birthday cake at a little party given him by the plant hospital and Personnel Depts." Marion Fulton is farthest to the left. Molly Quinlan is in the chair, front, center; Vincent Keville is to the right. *Janet Dempsey*

Many prizes awarded at Firth Carpet Company Annual Outing   Cornwall Local, 8/'58

Children's events

50 yard dash: Boys 7-12: Robert Walker; girls 8-12: Alice Menga; Boys 13-16: Joe Szulewski; Girls 13-16: Lou Kennedy.

Obstacle race: Boys 8-12: Joe Walker; Girls 8-12: Marlyn Moulder; Boys 13-16: George Burger; girls 13-16: Nancy Staples.

3 legged race: Boys: 8-12: Billy Ball and Ricky Wojehowski; Girls 8-12: Sharon Soukup and Marlyn Moulder; Boys 13-16: Joe Oljniczak; Girls 13-16: Judy Palermo and Diana Dickman.

Shoe race: Boys 8-12: Tommy Pindar; Girls 8-12; Alice Menga; Boys 8-12: Zig Olejniczak; Girls 8-12: Irene Olejniczak

Wheelbarrow race: Boys 8-12: Zig and Stan Olejniczak; Girls 8-12: Judy Palermo and Diana Dickman.

Balloon Race: Girls 8-12: Joan Burger; Boys 8-12: Bruce Walker.

Pie eating contest: Girls 8-12: Irene Olejniczak; Boys 8-12: George Burger.

Donkey contest: Boys 1-4: Robert Docherty; Boys 1-4: Gordon Stevenson; Girls 1-4: Roxana Satterly; Girls 1-4: Linda Gardner.

Children's races: Boys 5-7: Pat Eadry; Boys 5-7: Tommy Olejniczak; Girls 5-7: Joan Ward; Girls 5-7: Eileen Ann McGuiness.

Adult events

The race: Men: Egon Flgalski; Women: Katherine Flgalski;

Shoe race: Women: Carol Pillus.

3 legged race: Men: Vince and Jo Keville, 1st women, Ernest and Charlotte Burger, 2nd.

Needle and thread race: Men: John Horey; Women: Mabel Cox.

Sack race: Pat Eisloeffel.

Tug of war: Men: Harry Marshall, Wilson Hinkley, Bill Secor, Jim Quakenbush, Stanley Wierzbcki; Women: Agnes Rogers, Jennie Burger, Charlotte Burger, Helen Walker, Mabel Cox and Bertha Blaison.

Costume race: Men: 1st Mickey Olejniczak, 2nd; Stanley Wierzbicki Jr.

Beauty contest: Women; 1st; Joyce Ruskiewicz, 2nd, Carol Lawrence.

60 yard dash: Men: Stanley Wierzbicki Jr.; fat men's, Charlie Decker

Rolling pin contest: Women: Bertha Blaison and Jane O'Dell.

Horseshoe pitching: Women: Pearl Sieczek, Ethel Keegan, Mabel Cox and Helen Walker; Men: Jimmie Hunter, Bart Menga, Raymond O'Dell and John Keegan.

Special prizes

Long service: Men: Harrison O'Dell; Women: Sadie Quick

Long Service, retired: Man: Alex Sharpe; Women: Bertha Woolsey.

Oldest in age, retired: Man: Walter Cornell; Woman: Annie Redfern.

Oldest at outing: Man: Theodore Conklin; Women: Charlotte Masten.

Bean guessing: Man, Raymond O'Dell; Woman: Mae Johnson.

Attendance: Man, Archie Dunlap; Man: James Rider; Woman: Stella Smith; Woman: Mary Quinlan.

Committee prize: Man: Leon Hunter; Man, Henry Gildersleeve; Woman: Mary Mitchell; Woman: Grace Green.

Bingo Prizes

May Macdonald, Mae Johnson, John Krol, Jim Joslin, Theresa Olejniczak, Harry Smith, Conrad Stenglein, Mildred Rapoli, Clarence Ball, Helen Ross, Carl O'Dell, Barbara Quicksell, Mary Porter, Newt Staples, Zina Lopristi, Mickey Olejniczak, Josephine Ruggiero, Anna Ruggiero, Mabel Cormier, Betty Wands, Rose Paraio, Carmine Pettine, May Partridge, Ethel John, Jean Wierzbicki, Harold Perry.

END

June, 1957

".........The Firth Carpet Company is proud to congratulate the Lions Club on its 25th anniversary and it congratulates them on the fine work they have done for children and grownups alike. Just as the Lions club constantly drives to improve the life within the community and the services rendered to it, so does the Firth Carpet Company, as one of the five largest in its field of carpet making in the United States, drive to push forward the development and research by improved working conditions and by becoming an integral part of its community...."

Abridged version of longer article

Both, Cornwall Local, Cornwall Public Library

Next two pages: Firth employees   *George Kane*

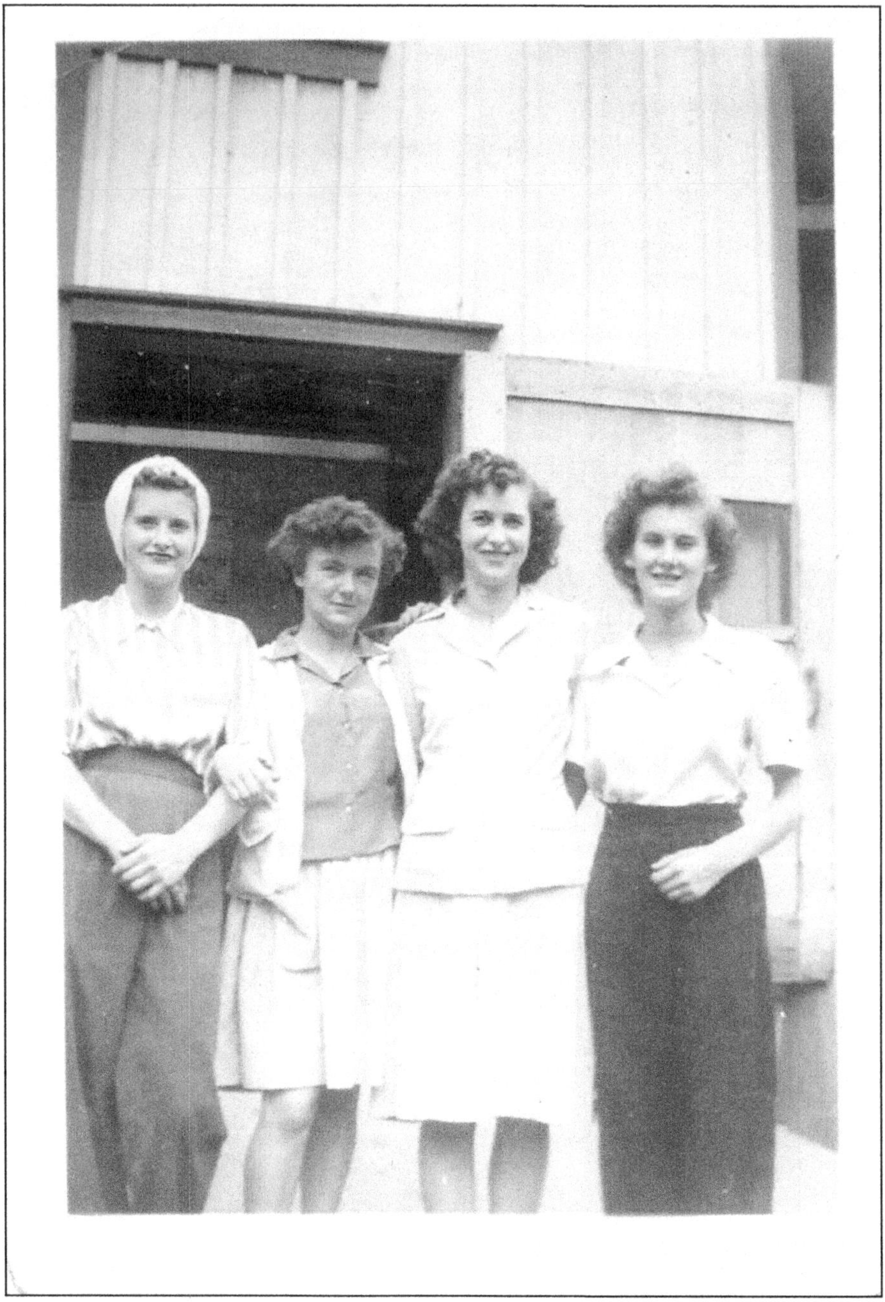

Tug of War, Firth Annual Picnic

1952

George Kane

Next four pages: Firth Company picnic, an annual summer tradition in good times and bad right through the last years of Firth Carpet.

May 7, 1953: Firth Carpet's charter amended to allow manufacture of goods other than carpets.

August, 5th, 1954: Firth starts to feel effects of high production costs and reduced demand. Sales drop more than a million dollars.

August, 1958: Closing of Wilton Division in Newburgh

Firth Carpet Picnic, Firthcliffe, NY Aug 12, 1944

Helen Evans, Pat Ross, Jane Samerjack, Pat Callahan, Howard Litchfield, Howard's Wife

Firth Carpet Picnic, Firthcliffe, NY Aug 12, 1944

Ross Sisters
Pat Ross
Helen Evans
Helen
O'Shaughnessy
Ann
Tommy
Margaret McKinesty
Flo Di Gorio
Virginia Tricarico
Evelyn Moore
Louella Quick
Audrey Ross
Harold Appleby
Tom Ross
Mollie Quinlan
Jerry
Jane Semick
Stella Neverleski
Edith Antalek
3

Firth Carpet Finishing Room
1943-1944

Firthcliffe, NY

Mr. Young
Mollie McOuistion
Stella Neveliski
Herb Ball
Gertrude Mae Tricarico
Minnie Shaw
Jerry
Edith Antalek
Harold
Elida Thompson
Sisters
Patsy Ross
Dorman
Walt Gordon
Walt Kirk
Margaret Hunter
Helen
Lula Quick
Virginia Tricarico
Bertha Woolsey
Susie
Claude
Jack
Walt

234

How did they take the company picnic photo?

Cover of the Firth News for July, 1957

Left to right on the cover are: David Parrella, Mike Raab doing the churning, Mildred Raab, Ivy Stewart and Victoria Parrella quilting, Al Hopkins rocking a baby in the cradle and Nicholas Parrella weaving rag rugs on a hand loom *Michael Raab*

THE FIRTH NEWS

Vol. XVIII   July 1957   No. 12

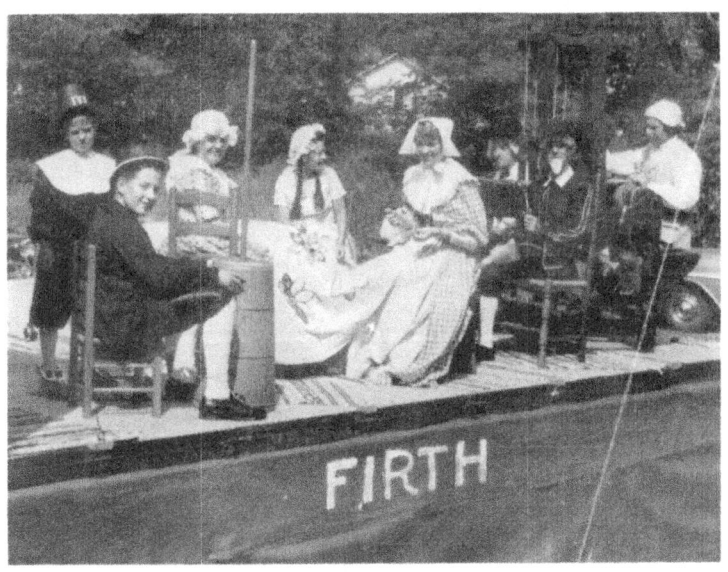

FIRTH FLOAT
In the Independence Day Celebration

1957 and 2019

Fourth of July, 2019

LLOYD CONKLIN — is a graduate of Washingtonville Central School — his mother, Dorothy, is employed in the Twisting Dept.

SPINNING DEPT.
by Jean Ball

Vacation time has rolled around again. By the time this issue is out everyone will be back hard at work. I hope you all had a wonderful time.

A new member among us is Bob Burnett. Bob is an excellent "harmonica" player. Someday we hope to see him on the Ted Mack Show.

Steve Dembeck and Casey Kusek went fishing the other night. I guess Steve decided to go for a swim, but forgot to take his clothes off.

Joe Pawelek is driving a different car now.

Carlo Patane spent one Sunday down at Coney Island — some of those rides nearly got him down.

Doris Baker and "Cap" O'Dell really had quite a time at Doris' niece's wedding recently.

Wonder if it's true that wedding bells are going to ring pretty soon for a cute young couple in our department?

Bill Pryne attended the graduation exercises at the Cornwall Central School. His daughter, Joyce, was a member of the graduating class.

Cap O'Dell and his son went to the Yankee Stadium on the Fourth of July.

CALLING CARDS
Betty Lobdell & John Doering

When we return from vacation this news will be waiting for us. There doesn't seem to be too much right now with everyone planning vacation and so on.

First, congratulations to Mr. and Mrs. Ed Reagan, who recently celebrated their 30th Wedding Anniversary with a big party in Yonkers; all their children attended.

Norman and Dot Howard also celebrated their 8th anniversary in July — best of luck.

Oh, by the way, did you know Bo-Bo likes ice cream or is it because Bill Logan sells it.

There was a very nice parade in Cornwall on July 4th — Firth had a nice float and if anyone happened to see the nice old lady running the spinning wheel, it was our own George Raab. I didn't know you could spin, George.

Bill Hinkley and Alvin Clark were "Confederate" soldiers in the same parade.

Ed Reagan and family have taken up residence in Firthcliffe. Better watch out, Ed, John Doering lives close by.

By the time this issue is out, Dominick Casalinuovo and his wife will be on the "high seas" bound for Italy. Have a good time and don't get seasick.

Well, folks, that is all the news for now. Have a good vacation.

SHIRLEY EELS — Her father, who is employed in our Carding Dept., told us she caused considerable commotion on Bridge Street, Cornwall, when she locked her mother in the chicken coop.

In the late 1950's, change was coming to the American economy, and not for the better, as the following letter on the following pages shows:

Problems of little man grow

By George Sokolsky

When Andrew Jackson fought the Bank of the United States, he was expressing the sentiment of the farmer against the stranglehold on the circulation of money by the banking powers, then most of them represented by the Biddles of Philadelphia.

THE SAME POWER exists today in a cartel of bankers, brokers, heads of life insurance companies, of mutuals and labor pension funds who put firms together in mergers, who take firms apart to benefit from the book values and market values, and take apart values; who sit on numerous boards of directors so that by interlocking directorships or by other group activities, they dominate the policies of a company or even an entire industry.

The peril to the country is that they are killing off the smaller manufacturer and the smaller distributors and are into the proletariat where they become an element of dissatisfaction and protest.

I have often written on this subject because I am convinced that the greatest peril to American capitalism is the concentration of the control of money. Now that I find that the Rockefeller Report "The challenge to America; It's economic and Social aspects" reaches much of the same conclusion, to wit: (Continues)

"There is...a growing body of evidence that smaller and medium businesses, and particularly manufacturing firms-even those that have successfully established themselves in their industries and have solid prospects for growth, have difficulty in obtaining financing for the expansion of their operations. There is also a probability that inadequate financing reduces the rate at which new firms are established.

The need is primarily for long term equity of loan funds. As a result of the inability to obtain capital funds, the opportunity for establishing a new firm, or expanding an established firm, is too often lost. Often the established firm merges with a larger enterprise that can command the necessary resources. The past few years have seen a wave of such mergers. Such a condition is neither conducive to vigorous competition nor to economic growth."

EVEN MORE than the economic consequences of this trend toward the elimination of the small producer and distributor are the social consequences that emanate there from.

Management in large enterprise is most likely to be divorced from ownership so that the salaried man and wage earner are only different in degree, whereas an owner of a property has more than a temporary interest in it; to him it is often a vested interest to which he is emotionally bound and which he seeks to preserve. His attitude towards his country is likely to be the same as toward his enterprise, namely a mingling of pride with a strong sense of preservation.

Ownership is psychologically different from unprotected management and produces different kind of person. In the up building stage of a capitalistic society, it is ownership that manages and that builds. In the down-going stage competition lessens and then mergers increase. It has then that the small man of great initiative loses his incentives and becomes static.

Evening News, February 2, 1958

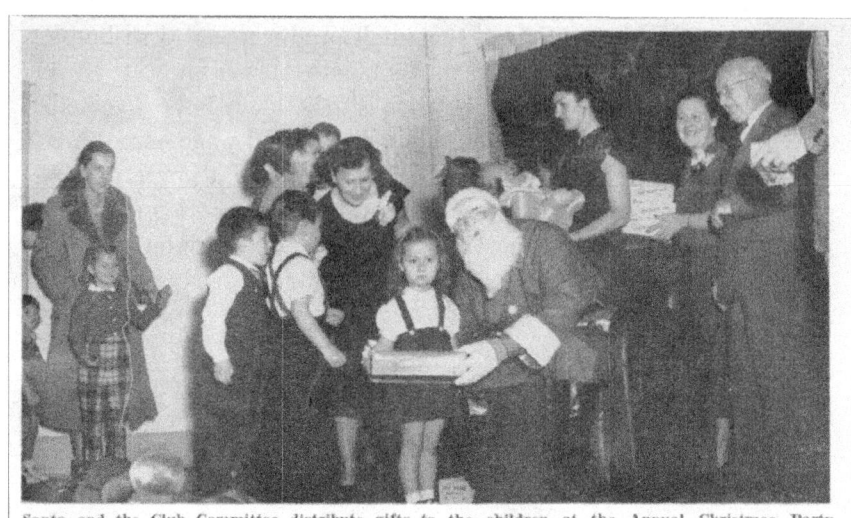

Santa and the Club Committee distribute gifts to the children at the Annual Christmas Party held in the Firthcliffe Club.

Firth Clubhouse Christmas Party, 1953
The boy to the left (above) is George Barley   *George Kane*

Christmas Shopping Center at Firth Clubhouse on Thursday and Friday

The Christmas Shopping Center sponsored by the Cornwall Post American Legion Auxiliary will be held at the Firthcliffe Club on Thursday, Dec. 11, and Friday, Dec. 12. All the Cornwall Merchants are participating. This is the only money making project of the Legion Auxiliary. Santa Claus will be on hand to greet the children. A surprise will be given to each child that greets Santa and tells him what they want for Christmas.

Door prizes will be awarded each evening. One does not have to be present to win. Booths will be on display and some of the articles for sale are: Toys, dolls, candy, fruit cakes, plastic wares, stationery, cosmetics, Christmas, ribbons, wrapping paper, jewelry, stockings, scarfs, collars, men's and boy's flannel shirts, house dresses, electrical appliances, Christmas cards, refreshments, men's wallets and many more items.

Get the Cornwall Holiday Spirit — Buy at the Center — Bargains Galore.

Merchants and organizations participating are: Highland Fling, Cornwall Delicatessen, Cerasoli's TV and Appliance Store, Hazards Pharmacy, Hey's Gifts and Appliances, Glube's Variety Store, Edgar's Wearing Apparel, Cohen's Fair Store, Ushman Brothers, Inc., Hardware, C. E. Cocks' Sons Grocers, Whitney's Pharmacy, St. John's Episcopal Church, Women's Society, Lillicotch's Christmas Candles, Ann's Beauty Shop, Ruth O. Kranz Antiques, McCoy Sales, Rebekah Trinity Lodge, Stanley Products, Ruth Hunter, Stanley Products, Mary Peleshuck, Santoro Bros. and Son Conf., Schofield Market, Clark's Market, U. Grant Clark's Market.

Cornwall Local/Cornwall Historical Society

August, 31, 1961: Merger with Mohasco Industries first proposed.

History of Mohasco Industries, which would purchase Firth Carpet

The company was founded in 1878 by four brothers in the Shuttleworth family. That year, the family shipped 14 used Wilton looms from Great Britain to Amsterdam, New York, and launched their own carpet mill. At the time, New England, with its corresponding emphasis on textile mills, was the carpet capital of the nation. For most of its history, Mohawk and its competitors wove floor coverings from wool, a naturally water-repellent and insulating fiber. In fact, little about the industry changed from the time of the invention of the power loom in the mid-19th century until after World War II. Even with mechanization, carpetmaking was a highly labor-intensive prospect using massive, complicated machinery. Manufacturers' dependence on unpredictable wool production added another variable to the equation, making for steep fluctuations in expenses. For most families, carpeting was an expensive luxury, so costly that per household shipments peaked at four square yards in 1899 and did not exceed that mark until the mid-1960s.

The Shuttleworth family business was not incorporated until a generational shift in leadership probably precipitated the move in 1902, when the company became known as Shuttleworth Brothers Company. The firm's reputation grew substantially after 1908, when it introduced the Karnak carpet pattern. This new style was so popular that a company history noted: "Weavers worked four and five years without changing either the color or the pattern on their looms."

Three generations of Shuttleworths dominated the carpet mill's first century in business. In 1920, they guided the first of what would become many mergers and acquisitions. That year, the family combined its firm with carpetmakers McCleary, Wallin and Crouse to form a leading force in the then fragmented industry. Renamed Mohawk Carpet Mills, Inc., the company was the country's only weaver with a full line of domestic carpets, encompassing the Wilton, Axminster, Velvet, and Chenille weaves. Mohawk did not rest on its laurels, creating the industry's first textured design, Shuttlepoint; the first sculptured weave, Raleigh; and Woven Interlock, "the first successful application of the knitting principle to the manufacture of carpet."

Postwar Era Brings Rapid Change

Several trends converged in the 1950s to reshape the carpet industry drastically. Wartime restrictions on the use of wool fueled research into alternative fibers, especially petrochemical-based synthetics including nylon and, later, acrylics. These man-made materials were much cheaper to produce and the supply was much more consistent than that of wool. At the same time, a revolution in the main weaving methods was underway. (Continues)

The new technique found its origins in Dalton, Georgia, which boasted a thriving cottage industry in tufted coverlets. In the late 1940s, housewives there had built up something of a tourist-trap industry in tufted bedspreads.

Machines were soon developed to tuft carpets by the same process-- inserting loops of fiber into a jute backing. These broadlooms could manufacture carpet many times faster than previous methods. Faster manufacturing methods, combined with the new materials developed in the ensuing decades, made the now familiar tufted carpets inexpensive and popular. By 1968, tufted carpeting accounted for 90 percent of all carpet sales.

In 1956, Mohawk merged with Alexander Smith, Inc. to form Mohasco Industries. Though the acquisition made Mohasco the world's largest carpet company, it proved to be poorly timed. The troubled Alexander Smith brought with it a high level of debt and a large inventory of outdated carpeting at a time when competition from imports was gaining steam. Tariff relaxations during the 1950s increased importers' share of the U.S. industry from 2 percent to 25 percent by the end of the decade. At the same time, Mohasco was compelled by industry imperatives to consolidate its mills in the South. Notwithstanding these problems, Mohasco President Herbert L. Shuttleworth II, the third and last of the family to lead the business, was able to stabilize the business enough to purchase high-ranking Firth Carpet in 1962.

From Mohasco's Website, Google search

The flowing collection of headlines tells the final story of Firth Carpet,

"PROPOSED SALE OF FIRTH CARPET CO. BY MOHASCO IS BLOCKED"   *Wednesday, January 2, 1961*

At the time Firth owed its creditors $5,528,000 and was encouraging the merger. As the stockholders met in New York to consider the merger and hoping to fend off the inevitable, Distributors were looking for a guarantee that the Firth line would continue.

"STOCKHOLDERS OF FIRTH WILL MEET TO CONSIDER MERGER WITH MOHASCO"   *January 17, 1962*

"MOHASCO MAKES ARRAGEMENTS FOR TRANSFER OF SOME OF FIRTH OPERATIONS"

February 15, 1962

The ball field was sold to John and Robert Fanning for $50,000. The club was sold The Cornwall Hospital, who later sold it to the Marci's, who operated a restaurant there until the club was destroyed by fire on October 26th, 1970.

"AHEN CLAIMS MOHASCO MERGER WITH FIRTH CARPET WAS FOR TAX ADVANTAGE" *February, 1962*

John Ahen was a Cornwall Trustee and was not running for reelection and "had no ax to grind" put the question to Mohasco concerning the fate of Firth carpet. At the time, Donald B. Tansil, Firth President, said the mill had losses of nearly 4 million in the 24 months ending Dec. 30, 1961.

The following article, the sale of Firth Carpet by Mohasco, ended the era of Firth Carpet in Firthcliffe and began the Era of Majestic Weaving, who would operate the plant until it's closing in the early 1980's. *Evening News 2/'63*

Firth Plant Sold

While area officials continue to look for a good tenant for the former Stroock plant in West Newburgh, it is encouraging to learn that the Firth Carpet plant in Cornwall has been sold to a New Jersey industry for $600,000. This is the figure set by Mohasco, which purchased the Firth plant a few years ago and eventually closed it down.

Full information is not available yet about the new owner, but readiness to pay such a substantial sum for the property is indicative that the firm is prepared to put it to good use. That means jobs and new people in the area, with the accompanying demand for housing and the merchandise which they will require.

There also should be some stability in such a substantial operation. Industry is not likely to move soon when it goes to such expense to locate in a new community.

Scant as it is, the news is good. Both for Cornwall and for the Newburgh community which once supplied so many workers for the big Firth plant.

TOO LATE

"President Kennedy's increase of the carpet tariff from 21 percent to 40 percent left a trail of confusion on both sides of the Atlantic last week.

Berlin and English concerns who sell millions of dollars worth of carpets to the U.S. each year are indignant over the President's maneuver. Like the rest of the world they have watched and believed his steady battle for liberalized trade policy. Last week they found him reversing his course to their great disadvantage.

Americans too, are confused. Many of them have been trying to persuade themselves that the President's direction towards freer trade is the country's only recourse in an ever shrinking world. They have followed his all-out efforts to persuade members of Congress to give him much stronger power than he has to stimulate trade by cutting tariffs. Suddenly, in the midst of this, Mr. Kennedy took the recommendation of the tariff commission and almost doubled the protection on carpets and glass.

The purpose of the move appears to be to persuade those who oppose a liberal free trade policy that the President takes the "escape clause" seriously. This clause (which would be continued in the President's new Trade Bill) allows tariff relief for an industry hurt by imports.

But the protection comes too late to help firms like Firth that have had to merge with larger companies because they could not meet the foreign competition. If the "escape clause" is applied only after factories are closed and workers are laid off, it will be of little help to American business. Meanwhile, the President's move has led Europe to question whether he is serious about liberalizing free trade and Americans to question the value of an "escape clause" that is applied too late to do any good."

Evening News, March 19, 1963

*"When the last sons of the old mill
gaze upon Moodna's banks no more
May we still recall Firth Carpet and the "Hollow"
Happy days of yore*

Obituaries   Both, Evening News

Samuel Docherty, 75, of 13 Maple St. Cornwall, died suddenly of a heart seizure at his home on Saturday afternoon (Aug. 5, 1961) after returning from the annual Firth Carpet Company employees outing at the Firthcliffe recreation par

Mr. Docherty retired last June as Personnel manager of Firth Carpet Co. where he had been employed for 50 years. He had held his post since 1946.

The husband of Catherine Martin Docherty, he was born in Johnston, Scotland, on March 10, 1886. He came to the United States while he still in his teens and took up residence in Firthcliffe more than 50 years ago.

He was a member of St. Thomas Church, Cornwall and St. Thomas Church Holy Name Society; Highland Engine Company of Cornwall; Cornwall Lions Club and the Scottish Clan McLeod.

The funeral will take place from the Bevans Chapel, 337 Hudson Street, Cornwall on Hudson, and Tuesday at 9:15 a.m. At 10 a.m. a High Mass of requiem will be offered at St. Thomas Church. Internment by Toohey Brothers will be at St. Thomas Cemetery.

Abridged version of much longer article

Orr Dies: Lawyer and Civic leader

Walter S. Orr, 69, of Orrs Mills and New York City, died on Monday (Sept. 25, 1961) of a coronary thrombosis in New York Hospital.

He was a senior partner of the law firm of White and Case, 14 Wall Street, New York City, and had lived at 580 Park Avenue.

Mr. Orr was educated in Cornwall High School, where had been a member of the championship basketball team of 1910. He was graduated from Amherst College in 1912 and Columbia Law School in 1915. He joined White and Case firm after his admission to the bar and became a partner in 1925. He specialized in taxation and corporate law.

Mr. Orr was a director of the Firth Carpet Co. and the Registrar and Transfer Co. He was also a trustee and vice president of the Myron and Annabel Taylor Foundation and of the Frazer Jelke Foundation. He was formerly a trustee of Amherst College from 1940 to 1947 was former president of the Amherst Society of New

York. He was formerly a member of the board of trustees of Storm King School at Cornwall, and the Cornwall Hospital.

He is survived by his wife, Mrs. Shirley Nelson Orr. Ian K. Deane of Rock Tavern is Mr. Orr's stepson.

Funeral services will be held at noon on Thursday at St. Thomas Episcopal Church, Fifth Avenue.

John G. O'Dell Sr.
January 15, 1926 - July 3, 2019
Cornwall-on-Hudson, NY

John G. O'Dell Sr. of Cornwall-on-Hudson, NY, passed away on July 3, 2019 at home. He was 93 years old.

The son of the late Russell S. O'Dell of Highland Falls, and Bertha M. Fergusen of Cornwall, he was born on January 15, 1926 in Cornwall, NY.

John volunteered for Naval Service in 1944, choosing to serve rather than graduating from Cornwall High School. He proudly served his tour of duty as a Radioman on a minesweeper in the Pacific during World War II. Upon returning home, he married "Betty," the love of his life, beginning a 71 year adventure together.

He worked for the Firth Carpet Company, then went on to work as a printer's apprentice and printer at the Cornwall Press in Cornwall-on-Hudson until it closed in 1975. He then worked for the Village of Cornwall-on-Hudson Highway Department until his retirement in 1987.

Known affectionately to his family as "Big Gramp", he shared his athletic and musical talents with his children. He took pride in being part of the six generations of O'Dells who have lived in the Cornwall community..."

Times Herald Record

THURSDAY, MAY 16, 1963

TOP SCORE HOLDERS: Albie Haight (left) and Bea Coddington were the top scoring team in the Firthcliffe Club Bowling League. Theron Lixfield had the highest average for the men and Miss Coddington had the highest average for the women.

McCue Family Holds Reunion

FAMILY REUNION—The McCue Family held a reunion at the Firthcliffe Club on Sunday afternoon. Attending were the children of the late Mr. and Mrs. Martin McCue of Cornwall, their children, grand children and great grand children, in addition to their wives and husbands. A total of 78 out of 123 relatives were at the reunion. Pictured in the front row, from left, to right, is John McCue, Martin McCue, Jr., Mrs. Ernest Smith, Mrs. George Arnott, Edward McCue and Joseph McCue. Standing left to right, are Robert McCue, and William McCue. Unable to attend were Mrs. Nathan LaBarr and Mrs. Jay Gould. Another child of the late Mr. and Mrs. McCue, Mrs. Edward DeMoss, is deceased.

80 Attend McCue Family Reunion Sunday

The McCue Family held a reunion at the Firthcliffe Club on Sunday, Oct. 25, when a buffet dinner was enjoyed.

Approximately 80 persons attended the reunion. The immediate family numbers 123 some now living in New Jersey, Florida, Texas and Vermont.

Those attending were: Mr. and Mrs. Edward McCue of Mountainville and their children and grandchildren; Mr. and Mrs. John McCue of Cornwall and their daughter; Mr. and Mrs. William McCue of Cornwall and their children and grandchildren; Mr. and Mrs. Martin McCue of Cornwall and their children and grandchildren; Mr. and Mrs. Robert McCue of Cornwall and their daughter; Mr. and Mrs. Joseph McCue of Hawthorne, N. Y., and their children; Mr. and Mrs. Ernest Smith (the former Mae McCue) of Cornwall and their children and grandchildren; Mr. and Mrs. George Arnott (the former Emily McCue) of Cornwall-on-Hudson and their son.

Unable to attend were: Mr. and Mrs. Nathan La Barr (the former Nell McCue) of Cornwall; Mr. and

The McCue family holds their family
Reunion at the Firthcliffe club, 1968
I remember the reunions in our backyard as a child, but this one was fated to be their last reunion held at the old club.

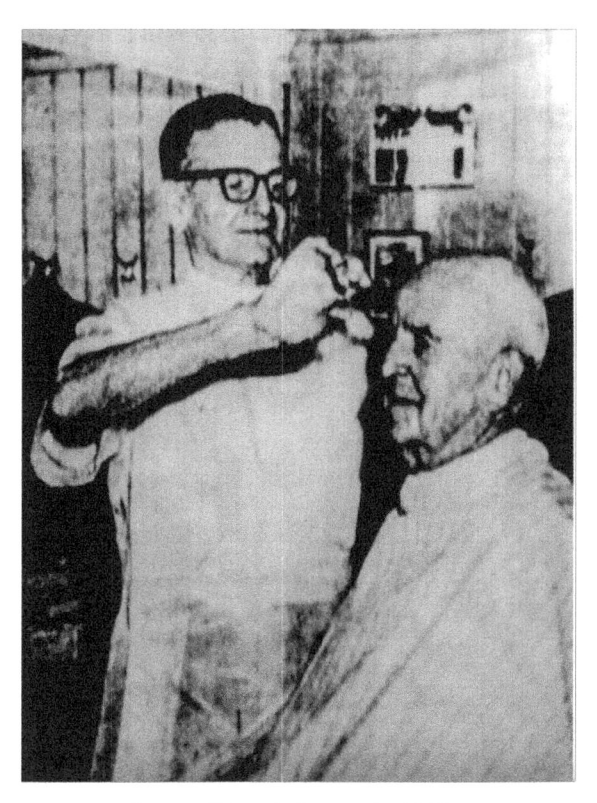

Cornwall Local, August 8, 1965:
"ONE OF THE LAST to have his hair cut by veteran Barber Bob Smith was Gustave O. Westlin of Willow Avenue.
Bob, who has maintained a Barber shop at the Firthcliffe Club since January 20, 1921, 44 and a half years, closed up shop Saturday and plans to at least partially retire. First he will take a long needed vacation and when he returns will continue to barber for shut-ins, the ill at home and those confined to the hospital. The clubhouse was acquired by Sal Marci last week for a restaurant and tavern. Mr. Westlin, also a well-known Cornwall resident, retired on December 1, 1963, after 35 years as a Mortician

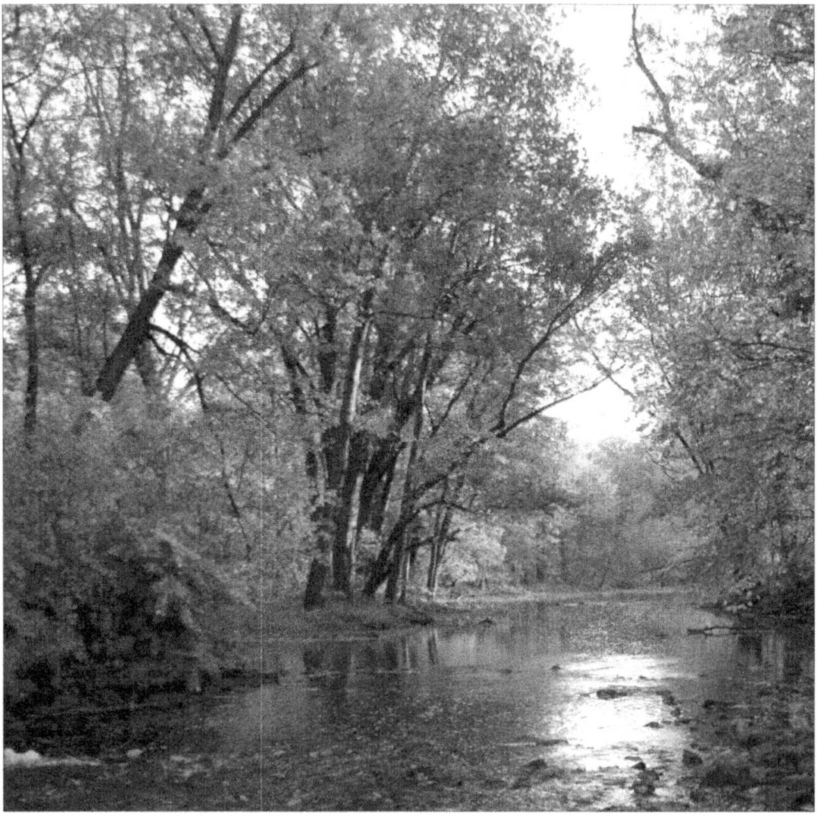

Chapter Fourteen:
A Moodna Farewell

In 1964 the pollution of Moodna Creek was so severe, as to inspire this poem from a member of the Black Rock Fish and Game club:

The Mockery of Moodna Creek

Grab your nose, slouch way down
Roll up the windows, mother
Were coming up to the Moodna Creek
It couldn't be another
The fish are dying-nay, there dead.
The health departments mighty sick
Or else they're are still a-bed
Mr. Mitchell's yelling loud
And all the sports clubs shriek
Mr. Becker tries his best
But still all ears are weak.
No one had realized before
The power paper swung-
Payola's license to defile
Sweet water-alas, unsung
Conservation's bogged way down
Right in the sludge with Health,
The only boys away on top are counting up their wealth.
So grab your pencil and defeat
Them with your very tools
Use YOUR PAPER-WRITE, WRITE, WRITE
And show them you're not fools.
Please help the ones who who've fought so hard
Get with it on their song
Or else the stench of Moodna will go merrily along.

Down along its journey and through time Moodna's waters have passed under no less than eleven bridges of three major railroad lines and at least that many highway bridges.*

This is only counting Moodna proper. It doesn't also take into account Woodbury, Otterkill and Idlewild.

Out of the ten railroad bridges that had once spanned these waters, I can count only two that are still in active service. Seven of them sit off in the woods, overgrown and forgotten. All that now remains of the O&W's bridge are concrete abutments, and is seeing its towering concrete footings toppled one by one by Moodna's seasonal wrath. The works of man will come and go, but Moodna Creek rolls forever on.

Footings for O&W'S Orrs Mills Trestle

The Bridge Builder

An old man, going a lone highway,
Came at the evening, cold and gray,
To chasm, vast and deep and wide,
Through which was flowing a sullen tide.
The old man crossed in the twilight dim;
The sullen stream had no fears for him;
But he turned when safe on the other side
And built a bridge to span the tide.
"Old man," said a fellow pilgrim near,
"You are wasting strength with building here;
Your journey will end with the ending day;
You never again must pass this way;
You have crossed the chasm, deep and wide --
Why build you the bridge at the eventide?"
The builder lifted his old gray head:
"Good friend, in the path I have come," he said,
"There followeth after me today
A youth whose feet must pass this way.
This chasm that has been naught to me
To that fair-haired youth may a pitfall be,
He, too, must cross in the twilight dim;
Good friend, I am building the bridge for him."
Will Allen Dromgoole

The Old Swinging Bridge

REMEMBER? - Only old timers will remember this, the swinging cable bridge over the Moodna Creek from the back of the Firth Carpet Buildings to the opposite side this was erected by Jim Aspinalls' maintenance crew for the workers who walked to work from Vails Gate. As Firthcliffe Heights built up they also used it. It was finally broken down by an ice jam in the 1920s but by that time most people drove to work so it was never replaced. When Cornwall was a dry town it is said many a pail of beer was carried across this bridge. We are told Claude Keator and the late Pat McKinstry are the men on the bridge.

5-6-71

(Photo loaned by George "Cal" Smith).

Near where The O&W crossed Mill Street lived this Firthcliffe resident that I remember seeing for many years.

Epilogue

And there used to be a ballpark, Where the field was warm and green….

...And the people played their crazy game with a joy I've never seen....

……..And the air was such a wonder, from the hotdogs to the beer

Yes, there used to be a ballpark right here……

And there used to be Rock Candy ....

…..And a great big Fourth of July….

.... With the fireworks exploding
all across a summer sky

And the people watched in wonder

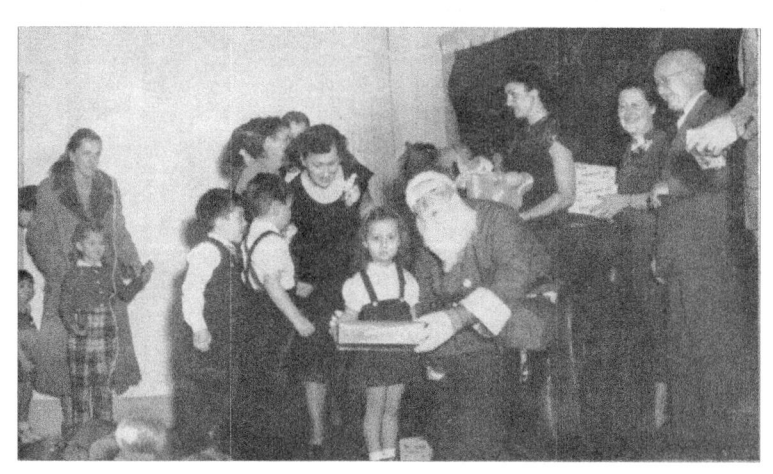

How they laughed, and how they cheered!

And there used to be a ballpark right here

Now the children try to find it...

And they can't believe
their eyes....

…..'cause the old team just isn't playing,

And the new team hardly tries

And the sky has got so cloudy,

When it used to be so clear

And the summer went so quickly, this year...

Yes, there used to be a ballpark...

......Right.... here......

Powerhouse, Firth Carpet

Made in United States
North Haven, CT
07 March 2023